Stories from the Thirty Birds

Published in 2023 by
Fons Vitae
49 Mockingbird Valley Drive
Louisville, KY 40207
http://www.fonsvitae.com
Email: fonsvitaeky@aol.com

Library of Congress Control Number: 2023946037

ISBN 978-1941610-954

Cover art by
Rafar Anwer, Creative Studio
Simorgh Exhibition of Seven Minatures,
Lahore, 2021

Printed in USA

Stories from the Thirty Birds

From "I" to Him

By
Hasan Kerim Guc

Translated by Hilal Tokat

FONS VITAE

CONTENTS

PREFACE

An unusual offering comes to us from the son of a living Turkish Spiritual Master, Cemalnur Sargut. Kerim Guc has selected stories from various cultures and epochs which have been a support to his own journey from "I" to "Him." These help to clarify 30 needed spiritual "realizations." He first sums up a version of the famed 12th century "Conference of the Birds" by Attar, in which 30 of the thousands of aspiring birds, who are making the treacherous Journey of Return to the Great Simurgh bird, succeed in reaching the Gate to The Divine Presence. Wisdom-Teachings are then presented in the form of 30 stories whose telling will hopefully succeed in opening the Immense Threshold, closed before them. Just as in the tale told by the Crane, in which it took tiny morsels of food contributed by villagers in a starving Irish town to make a nourishing soup that saved all their lives, each story shared by the 30 birds, one by one, helped to further open the Threshold to the Divine Source.

What makes this work unique and relevant to the world today is that these tales come from such a wide variety of sources – as distant as Hindu and Greek mythology and as near as words from the Turkish National poet, Yunus Emre, and Indigenous cultures of the Americas.

Just as a 10th century predecessor, The Animal's Lawsuit Against Humanity (written in Baghdad by the Ikhwan As-Sa-fa / Brethren of Purity) is as relative today with its concern for our environment and animal rights, Kerim Guc also addresses these same critical issues.

To further underscore the universality and timelessness of the points being made in this book, the text is ornamented with supportive quotations from world citizens dating back to Lao Tse, the Buddha, Seneca and St. Augustine. Further passages closer to our times were chosen from such luminaries as Martin Luther King, Ben Franklin, Kipling, Gandhi, Winston Churchill, and Nelson Mandela.

The tales, inspired by such a wide variety of times and cultures, illustrate for the reader important aspects of the perennial spiritual journey. They illustrate key virtues for the needed transformation.

To start with, three Companions of the Cave emphasize the need for filial piety, overcoming envy with generosity, and the importance of protecting what belongs to others. We look at the principle of Harmony which connects all humanity in peace – from the Flamingo's tale. The Swan takes us to tribal lands in the American West where in a magical story about the Flow, a Sioux youth finally realizes that he can trust the Divine to take care of everything. A most moving narrative from the Seagull takes place in modern day Istanbul where the greed of a Turkish businessman is contrasted with the inner contentment, joy and generosity of a poor lad who collects discarded paper with his meager pushcart. We are treated also in Turkey to the words of the 13th Century master mystic poet, Yunes Emre. The Robin, then, conveys to us his metaphor of the exemplary bee.

The Dove transports us to India where Vishnu, the Lord and Sustaining principle of the Universe, recognizes and praises a poor villager's humility and constant remembrance of the Divine. A person's purity of heart affects his perception. The Eagle demonstrates how true justice depends on this. An unusual story about Unity, from the Pheasant, takes place in 15th century Istanbul. It is based on a myth about the hyacinth flower popular in Ancient Greece.

We hear about the abuse of good fortune as well as the importance of both sacrifice and "putting the other first," from the Hawk and the Partridge. In an Australian Aboriginal tale, a Kangaroo teaches us about generosity. A Sufi teaching is delivered by the Stork in which we encounter the even-tempered character of a rich man whose fortune, however, alternates. His heart remains steadfast in the knowledge of the "temporariness" of every aspect of life. The Owl and Pigeon offer us wisdom from India: How the Saint Muinuddin Chisty first came to Agra and then how the Chisty saint, 300 years later, appeared to Sultan Akbar in a dream, leading the Sultan to a life of service to others. The 20th century Turkish Sufi Master, Ken'an Rifai, delivers a commentary on the contrast between Alexander the Great's ego with that of Diogenes. Following after the Falcon, the Peacock transports the reader to the world and wisdom of Lao Tse where the problem of being close -minded and distrustful is explored. We then learn how a special message from the Islamic mystic, al-Hallaj, was transmitted through a pick-pocket with whom he was imprisoned. The environment, compassion and humility are addressed, and then followed by a look at the alchemy that comes from experiencing true wealth as the absence of needs.

The "life of the living dead," explains the Swallow, arises if we have no struggles or trials but dwell in an otherwise deadening daily hum-drum. We can get imprisoned, each in our own cage, matrix or way of life. The Kite relates the narrative of Buddha's life and issues surrounding death. When the Crane described the nourishing soup made by the tiny "sharings" of the starving Irish villagers, she was pointing out how great strength arises from Unity. A further metaphor is given for when everyone is working equally together, that of the V formation of birds in flight. The momentary "leader" eases back when tired and another assumes his place. All serve equally.

We are counseled, "Don't leave anyone behind, cover each other's shortcomings!" Kerim Guc often uses stories that take place within other stories. This has the effect of reminding the reader that this is what is happening continuously in our lives. The stories of the final four birds, the Albatross, Crow, Nightingale and Tuti remind us to avoid suspicion and factless assumptions, to curtail our ego's craving for adulation and praise, to be forgiving like Jesus and have sincere Trust in God.

SPECIAL THANKS

To my other half Gamze Guc,

To three women who raised me: my grandma Meşkure Sargut, my mom Cemalnur Sargut and my aunt Asuman Sargut Kulaksız,

To my translator Hilal Tokat,

To my U.S.A publisher and editor Gray Henry and the Fons Vitae Team,

To my second editor Çiğdem Bozyürek,

To Tokat Family,

To my Turkish Publisher Tuti Team (Belgin Batum, Elif Hilal Doğan, Melik Uyar),

To my illustrator Ece Ünal,

To Rafay Anwer for the cover page,

To Sufi Corner...

Hasan Kerim Güç

*"Life is a story.
And to love a person is to love their story."*

Martin Heidegger

THE JOURNEY FROM "I" TO "HIM"

"I" am comprised of but a single vowel. But when I realized that I could not be the "best" in everything, I left "I" behind and started to follow the "trace" of "u" and "s" and found "us."

We were happy with "us" when suddenly "You" appeared.

As "us" and "You" came together, we began to speak. There were "words" between us.

Then we left, and You left too. Only "words" remained.

When we mentioned "words," we remembered the promise we had given such a long time ago that we had forgotten.

And then we recalled to Whom we had given that "promise."

That was when we encountered the "Essence." And that is when we recognized "Him."

"Am I not your Lord?"

"Yes. We bear witness."

"Lest on the Day of Reckoning you plead ignorance of this Covenant."

MY GRANDMOTHER'S STORIES

March 2021, Istanbul

My Dear friends,

I am one of the fortunate representatives of the generation raised by their grandmothers. Now, looking back at the past, I have a better understanding of this blessing. My grandmother would let me sleep next to her on the weekends we spent together; we had made it a habit to count the stars before bedtime. I remember a big window beside the bed, opening out to the entire sky... Or perhaps it was a window enlarged many times by the power of my untarnished imagination. It turns out that every star has its own story. My grandmother would tell me one of these stories every night. Giants, dwarfs, love, wars...

Now, when I look back, seemingly through an obscure tunnel covered by either years or roads, I see today's me looking enviously at that little me. The sediment that has accumulated on the filter of my coffee machine makes my morning coffee bitter, which tastes just like the hurtful bitterness that arises from the sediment of a life seeping through polluted conscience filters. When buying clothes, we always avoid buying white, don't we? Because we know that white gets dirty quickly. However, dark colors are risk-free; they don't show dirt. I realized that life has often dressed us in dark-colored clothes so that our innocence could be tarnished without our souls noticing.

As I indulged in memories, the little me seemed absolutely white to my eyes, with no reservations about addictions,

worries, causes, or consequences. I was free from all preju-
dices while listening to my grandmother's stories in her lap.
My grandmother's words continue to echo in my ears as if it
were yesterday:

**"In every story, there is a hidden truth. If you know
your story, you will find your truth."**

Today's "me," however, has turned its purposes into
means and means into purposes. It wanted to return to these
stories when it realised the truth had ceased to be genuine.
That's how the story of this book began.

These stories I have been listening to since childhood are
now my children who have siblings born from my imagination. They have come through different eras, different cultures, and different countries. When writing these tales, it
was the innocence of that little me that accompanied me
rather than the anxieties arising from today's me's values, or
at least that's how I felt. Now it's time to share them. Perhaps
one of these stories that enlighten me when I'm feeling down
will touch the heart of one of you. This will be the greatest
happiness for both that little me and today's me. If I have
made any mistakes in my use of the English language, I ask
for forgiveness.

THE GUIDE

The Hoopoe bird thought of all the meetings that had taken place so far. There was no doubt that this gathering would be more crowded than any before; The Realm of Birds was perhaps experiencing the most threatening period in its history. The birds, who had always managed to communicate with their relatives in the most remote corners of the world, were now horrified by the news of yet another species ceasing to exist every day. The rightful inhabitants of the world, who had lived together under the blue sky for hundreds of thousands of years were now facing eviction notices nearly daily.

Soon, following a tradition going back many, many years, the birds' assembly would reconvene once again. This was a meeting independent of Time and Space. Birds from the past and future and from both east and west would fly in to attend, hoping to find a solution to the threat they all faced. When the assembly was finally convened, first the ancient birds complained that humans, who had once graced this world as brethren of Nature, had turned their backs against their siblings in recent times. Speaking on the behalf of the elder birds, the Robin first took the floor and addressed this assembly:

"Every living being is born out of love. I have been living for thousands of years. I have seen fear, anxiety, sadness, envy, hope, all of them. I understood that at the end of the day, our essential state of being – love, always wins no matter which emotion pushes itself forward. Humans, however, are resisting the love which is central to their nature. Just think, what would someone who fights against his or her own nature do when it comes to his or her relation with *us*, their bird bretheren?

All the ancient birds nodded sadly in agreement with Robin's concerns. The younger birds had also witnessed the oppression inflicted by humans against Nature since being born. They were therefore in an even more desperate state as compared with the older generations. **"What can we do!** With each passing period of time, one of our species disappears!" Canary protested. "How can we remind people of Mercy if it, too, is forgotten?" it continued.

The Crow joined the conversation: "I witnessed the day when Cain killed his brother Abel. Throughout history, those who are like Cain, unable to live up to their words, have crushed those who, like Abel, are genuine and truly act upon their words. How can we teach Mercy where a brother does not show mercy to a brother?"

Then the Eagle spoke: "My brothers! No one among you knows better than I what to do in stormy weather. While you seek shelter in the rain, I soar above the clouds. Remember, what you see from below looks very different from what one sees from above." The Hoopoe agreed with the Eagle and said, "We need a Bird that can show us the bigger, Real picture."

The Partridge seemed to guess what the Hoopoe was about to say: "Oh, Hoopoe! Do not deceive us with mere tales. Do not attempt to bring up *that* Bird, which we have grown up hearing about only in legends for centuries... that is nothing more than a dream when it comes to our **salvation**! We cannot solve our **real** problems with imaginary heroes. Use your intellect!"

The Hoopoe cautiously responded to this criticism: "My dear brother, **who** among us can **truly** know what is imaginary and what is Real? Perhaps this is our greatest challenge. Looking at the state of humankind, who do not listen to their hearts, I invite you all to listen to **your own...**" The Hoopoe took a deep breath and continued: "All living beings are parts of a single core Reality. The more we abide in that core, the more alive we are. Humans have turned their backs on their very core essence. I suggest we have no choice but to return to **ours...**"

The Hoopoe was referring to a journey made to the legendary bird, the Simurgh, which no other bird had ever seen. The path there would be very difficult, and many birds would perish along the way. But this was clearly the only solution which could bring the birds back to their pure Heart essences. The majority of the birds in the assembly reluctantly accepted this proposal. The assembly granted the Hoopoe the authority to be their guide. And so it was that the challenging journey to reach Mount Qaf, the home of the Simurgh, began...

THE JOURNEY

The birds found themselves on a most unfamiliar route. With hope in one wing and fear in the other, they flapped their wings. Their efforts would continue until they reached a valley that resembled the Eden Paradise they had heard of in legends. When they landed, the Hoopoe gathered the birds around him to explain the significance of this valley: "My brothers, this is the Valley of Desire. Whatever you wish for in your imagination becomes real here. However, this place is no different from mirages in the desert. What you think is *real* is actually only fleeting, passing and transient; this is what you are mistakenly attached to in this world. Be your True Selves, use your Hearts and do not get fooled and caught up in temporary things."

As he spoke out, the Hoopoe sadly knew in his heart that most of his companions would not make it out of this valley. The Path to the Ultimate Truth is the path of those with a special aptitude, and they are few. And so it happened. More than half of the birds that had set out decided to stay in this valley, enjoying life's "passing show." The Hoopoe gathered those who would continue with him and set out once again.

When they reached the second valley along their route, the area was covered with fog. The Hoopoe addressed his companions as he had done in the previous valley, "My brothers and sisters! This is the Valley of Love. You will see reflections in the fog. These are but blurry images of the true objects which are worthy of your love. Do not be deceived by mistaking them for real..." However, some birds who saw these reflections were deceived and ended their journey, preferring to stay on. The Hoopoe smiled compassionately at those who would now be left behind and soared with the others into the sky.

While each of the valleys that they passed through had offered the birds an alluring and difficult-to-resist promise of some happiness, their third stop was the daunting Valley of Knowledge. This valley's attraction was its offer of knowledge. This offer was the most mind-boggling of all the offers encountered so far. Indeed, many birds, as the Hoopoe predicted, were deceived by the knowledge available to be had in this valley. Yes, knowledge is the most valuable treasure in the world, but there are two kinds - one outward and the other inward. Birds deceived by the attainment of the knowledge of worldly things would never be able to reach the Knowledge of the Heart and the very Source of *that* Knowledge.

The Hoopoe continued on with the few remaining birds. Destiny drew this weary group to a darkened Valley this time. There was no trace of the sun, no sign. The Hoopoe assembled the birds around him as he had done in each previous valley. Many birds, however, could no longer make the effort to even pay attention. Still, with all his strength, he shouted: "My brothers and sisters, I know you are very tired, but we have crossed halfway. I cannot tell you that the journey will become easier, but please do not lose hope." This valley they had reached was the Valley of Satiety, or satisfaction with the way things are. It whispered to the birds that the journey had no benefit. How much they had strained themselves for the truth! Yet, what good had the legendary Mount Qaf ever done for any bird, and would *now* do for them? Despair seemed to heavily weigh down the birds' wings, and many decided to stay in this valley.

The Hoopoe then flew with the remaining companions to the Valley of Unity. The birds who came with him experienced a certain kind of loneliness within the multitude, for the first time. The pleasure of drifting apart off on their own, of getting lost in this valley, was so overpowering that they could no longer hear the Hoopoe. The Hoopoe took the birds he could save from this valley to perhaps the biggest trial that was yet to come on the journey, the Valley of Astonishment. A great majority of the remaining few hundred birds fell victim to the lure of this valley which was filled with extraordinary beauty. After seeing what was in this valley, many birds lost their ability to move, as if enchanted. Only the handful of birds, who could turn away from these mesmerizing images and follow the Hoopoe, safely reached the final valley. This was the Valley of Annihilation. Only those whose lower natures could die before their physical death could pass through this valley. This valley was a gateway through which only those who could realize their nothingness, while still existing, could enter and pass. Only 30 birds managed to cross through this final threshold.

So, out of the thousands of birds that set out together, only 30 managed to overcome the distractions posed by the previous valleys as they approached the final portal. The Hoopoe began preparing his companions for this last leg of the journey. The peak of Mount Qaf was at last within visible distance for the birds. The Hoopoe had known of the challenges they would face in the prior valleys, but he had no idea what to do when they reached the summit of Mount Qaf. Despite everything, the excitement of meeting the Simurgh had removed all worries. The birds flew to the top of the mountain and found themselves in front of a massive door, almost as imposing as a small mountain. The Hoopoe realized that this door was the *only* barrier between them and the great Simurgh. If they could solve the final riddle for entrance, they would be able to pass through the threshold before them. The only clue for entrance they had was in the inscription on the door: "Every story leads to a Truth." As always, the Hoopoe consulted his never-failing Heart. The answer from the Hoopoe's heart arose and came out as the Story of Three Young men, the *Ashab al-Kahf,* or the Companions of the Cave.

Using the story of the *Ashab al-Kahf* as inspiration, the Hoopoe and the 30 birds came to understand that the key to unlocking the massive door was the realization that the Truth they sought was within themselves. With this revelation, the door could be opened, and they might enter a magnificent realm, and finally encounter the Simurgh. The Simurgh would reveal to them that their Journey had been one of Self-discovery and that each of them carried a piece of the truth within. United, they would be able to merge with the essence of the Simurgh, overwhelmed with joy and understanding. Later, the birds, with their newfound wisdom, would be able to return to the world, forever transformed by their journey through the valleys into the Presence of One. But the giant magnificent door still had yet to be opened!

THE STORY OF HOW THE DOOR
WAS FINALLY OPENED

Now that you have heard the joyful conclusion to the story of the birds' journey to Mount Qaf, it is time to hear stories, more relevant to today, to understand what the birds actually needed to *deeply* grasp, in order for the great door to the Simurgh to be at last opened. It took the realization of all 30 birds to gain entry into the magnificent Presence of the glorious Simurgh and discover the True Way that both birds - and people - must *be*. So in each of the 30 stories to follow, make note of the teachings which open our hearts to the Real.

"How good life is when one does something good and just!"

The Karamazov Brothers
- Fyodor Mikhailovich Dostoevsky

THE HOOPOE'S STORY
GOODNESS

During the time of the Israelites, three young men were caught in a great storm while traveling in the countryside. They barely managed to find shelter in a cave and so decided to wait there until the storm subsided. However, the storm was so fierce that it uprooted trees and carried them away. Within a short period of time, the waters moved a large rock and dragged it to the entrance of the cave, blocking it completely. The young men realized that they wouldn't be able to unblock the entrance with their own strength and became worried that they might never see the light of day again. After pondering what to do, they decided to rest due to exhaustion and cold. One of them suggested that they pray to God. However, the others objected, saying, "What good have we done in our lives that would make us worthy of God's help?" This question led them all to think. They became quiet and introspective. Then, each began to tell his or her own story.

The first of the three young men recounted, "I lived with my elderly parents for years. Every evening at home, I would personally give them milk to drink. I wouldn't even feed my wife or child until my parents had drunk their milk. Once, when I was late coming home from collecting firewood due to a rain-swollen river, I found my parents had fallen asleep without drinking their milk. My heart ached for leaving them hungry. I couldn't sleep and spent the night holding the two cups of milk. As soon as they woke up, I fed them and promised God never to leave them hungry again."

As this young man finished his story, the rock blocking the cave's entrance began to quiver with tremendous noise. But it stopped at a certain point. The second young man immediately began relating his own story:

"Last year, famine devastated our village. I was one of the few villagers who dealt with trade, so even during the famine, I had money. But the famine was much harder on my neighbor's family. He didn't have enough income to feed his wife and children. I brought them food a couple of times. To be honest, I was very envious of their beautiful children but could never admit it to myself. As I visited their home, my envy increased. My neighbor's wife must have sensed this and, with her maternal instincts, was willing to do anything to provide for her children. One day, when her husband was away, she came to my house to ask for a loan; my envy had cast a dark fog over my body, obscuring my conscience. But my regret for this quickly brought me to my senses. I apologized to her and began to cry. While repenting, I immediately gave her the money she needed."

When the story ended, the rock in front of the entrance moved a second time, making a roaring noise, and opened just enough to let sunlight in. Then the third young man told his story: "I had a field inherited from my father. In the spring, I would hire workers to plow the field. Once, one of the workers had to leave early because his wife fell ill, and he left without taking his pay. That day, I bought a lamb with the extra money. Years passed. It turned out the worker had lost his wife that day, and fate had dragged him from place to place. When he finally returned years later, he asked for his rightful pay. I showed him the flock guarded by two shepherd dogs and said, 'You can take them; they're yours.' The worker was bewildered, 'How can that be? I only worked for you for one day...' But the lamb bought with his wages had grown, given birth, and its offspring had also given birth. Over the years, a single lamb had turned into a large flock. As the third young man finished his story and said, "Would I ever lay a hand on his rights?", the rock started rolling, and the entrance to the cave opened even further.

When Hoopoe finished his story, the enormous door on the summit of Mount Qaf had opened enough to astonish the birds. Hoopoe had fulfilled his duty having guided the birds on the Path of Goodness. His heart did not betray him, and the final mystery was being unraveled. Each of the 30 birds would understand and tell his or her own story. The Simurgh would then open the Door of Reality - the Door of Truth, a little bit more with each genuine tale. When the last story would be told, the birds hoped to encounter The Glorious Simurgh.

The Hoopoe bowed his head before the door, indicating that it was time for the next bird to share his or her story.

"And this is the eternal law.
For, Evil often stops short at itself and dies
with the doer of it! but Good, never."

Our Mutual Friend - Charles Dickens

-2-
THE FLAMINGO'S STORY
HARMONY

*"You are only afraid if you are not
in harmony with yourself"*

Hermann Hesse

The word "philharmony" comes from the Greek words "philo," meaning to love, and "harmony." Harmony is one of the things that resonate most with the human soul. No wonder harmony is a miracle created by the combination of seven notes in what we call music. To answer the question of where these notes come from and how they were born, let us take you to the story of a life born from two deaths...

It was only a few years before the world reached its era of Anno Domini. Elisa, or Elizabeth, a descendant of Aaron the brother of Moses, one of the most honorable families mentioned in the Holy Scriptures, had married the Priest Zechariah. This marriage laid the groundwork for a series of events that would profoundly affect the spirituality of the world. Elisa's cousin was Mary, who would represent the exalted position of motherhood. Mary was still in her mother's womb when her father Imran passed away. With Zechariah taking on the guardianship of young Mary, the flawless wheels of destiny began to turn.

The family had actually been expecting a baby boy, and they planned for this boy to serve in the temple. However, Mary was born instead of the expected son; she was different from other children even at a young age. As she grew up, it became more apparent that purity and beauty were like a garment sewn for her. She eventually became the first girl to have the honor of serving the temple.

Zechariah developed a habit of bringing food to his adopted daughter in the sanctuary every day. He loved her dearly, but it was unclear whether his love also stemmed from longing for a child of his own. Both Zechariah and Elisa were nearing the end of their century-long lives and had accepted that they could no longer have a child.

During one of Zechariah's regular visits to the temple, Mary offered him heavenly fruits unlike any found on earth. Zechariah was captivated by the beauty of what food he beheld and was unable to hide his amazement. He asked from whence this food had come. Mary spoke the words shared by all the Holy Scriptures, "From God. For God provides sustenance to whom He pleases without measure." "There is no difficulty for the Creator." In essence, Mary was proclaiming, "God gives directly to those who give of themselves." At that moment, Zechariah prayed that the lord grant his request for a child of his own.

Zechariah knew that he and his wife, Elisa, were nearing their time to depart from this world. He thought it was impossible for life to emerge from two dying people until that conversation with Mary. After hearing her words, he wondered why he had never considered the power of his Creator to make anything possible.

It has been noted that without hope, the unexpected cannot be found. Zechariah's faith and prayer would quickly turn into reality. With the seed of prayer planted that day, "life" emerged from "two deaths," and the child was named "John." This name was derived from the Arabic phrase "Ya Hayy," meaning "the living one," and had never been heard before in Jewish families as the name of one of God's elect. Six months after John's birth, his cousin Mary gave birth to Jesus Christ, who would change the course of the world, and John would accompany him.

Returning to the love of harmony, a thousand years after John, who has been referred to as the symbol of resurrection, an Italian priest in the Tuscany Valley discovered the secrets of modern music in John's verses. In his famous verses, John said:

Ut queant laxis

Resonāre fibris

Mira gestorum

Famuli tuorum,

Solve polluti

Labii reatum,

Sancte Iohannes

The priest, named Guido, discovered the letters of a hidden language that formed the harmony of life with the first syllable of each verse in this hymn, which said, "Let miracles find resonance in loose strings then, cleanse the stain on the lips of your servants, O Saint John!" These syllables were ut, re, mi, fa, sol, la, and si. The first note of this divine alphabet, ut, was later replaced with 'do', a contraction derived from "dominus," meaning "absolute being."

In a world based on the perception of changes by the senses, humankind was not capable of perceiving either a color or a sound on its own. Therefore, the Creator tested his creations with combinations of multiplicity. Just as divine light was divided into seven colors in this world, divine sound also found life in this world through seven different notes. As John said, with these seven notes, mankind would perform miracles while purifying their souls by their manner of speech.

All of humanity loves harmony, whether being aware of it or not. In other words, together they are creating a symphony. People are alive to the extent that they are a part of this harmony.

It has also been said, ***"Music, or harmony, is the language of the soul; it is what ends conflict and brings peace, unraveling the mystery of life."***

Thus, as the Flamingo finished its story,
the birds saw the door stirring slightly...

"The flow is mysterious. It's like a muscle:
The more you exercise it, the more it flows."

Ikigai – Francesc Miralles

3

THE SWAN'S STORY
FLOW

Tyee had not found the time to think about what he needed to bring with him before setting off on his journey. He guessed the place to which he was going would be cold. Since his wife departed, he had not been able to maintain order in the house. Denver was usually cold this time of year, and the place to which he was heading was five hours further north. When his grandfather was alive, he used to tell Tyee stories about the Cheyenne River camp every night. This was the tale of the white man forcing the Sioux to live in an area of 11,000 square kilometers in the world's largest open-air prison, and the stories had been passed down from generation to generation since the early 1900s. Tyee was the last of his generation of Sioux who had grown up with white people, and to be honest, he had never been interested in his ancestors' painful history. But the pain he had experienced in the last few months had left him feeling so helpless that he had come to seek solace in old wives' tales. Tyee had finally been convinced by his cousin that he could be a healer in the ancestral lands, which he had only visited a few times on short trips.

Tyee stuffed the first few sweaters he found in the closet of winter clothes into his duffel bag. He thought that he would only be staying at the camp for a few days anyway. If necessary, he could buy a few items from a nearby settlement. He couldn't afford to waste any more time. Although he had a hard time admitting it to himself, this journey might be his last chance before crossing the point of no return. As he walked towards his truck, he glanced at the mailbox, secretly hoping to find a letter from his wife, who had left home. When he opened the mailbox, he expected to find a letter saying that everything would be fine... Instead, he found a court paper notifying him of eviction from his home. He had spent the last six months unemployed and, like many Americans, had completely depleted his budget by stretching to buy the largest house he could. It's the nature of capitalism; everything you buy with the intention of owning eventually ends up owning you. Tyee couldn't help but think it was a bit late for realizing this as he set off with the gently falling snow.

By the time Tyee reached the camp, it was beginning to get dark. He tried to find the address his cousin had given him, as his phone's navigation feature simultaneously no longer functioned in this area. Despite being miles away from civilization, an unexpected wave of happiness was rising within him. For the first time, Tyee felt genuinely at home. He had only visited a few times when he was little. His uncle Payteh, who must have been over seventy years old, greeted his nephew at the entrance of the camp, in front of the huts. At first, Tyee was surprised by his uncle's long, braided hair and unexpected athletic body for his age. Tyee found it strange that his uncle still wore traditional clothes, but at the same time, he thought it didn't matter what he wore in this remote place.

In the Sioux tribe, as in other indigenous tribes, the male child held a very significant place. Tyee was the firstborn son of the family, and all family members felt great joy at his birth. The literal meaning of Tyee was "chief," and his family honored him with this name as the firstborn son. The one who suggested the name was none other than his uncle Paytah. In fact, his uncle had always followed this boy from a distance, perhaps waiting for this day. Unless a Sioux returns home by his own will, no other Sioux can interfere. Now Paytah's nephew needed his help for the first time.

Paytah took Tyee to his tent. The heavy, unusual smell Tyee noticed as they sat on the ground suggested that incense had been burned inside recently. As he inhaled this peculiar scent, he tried to understand how a simple Native American tent could be so warm in the middle of winter. From the moment he entered the camp, he was in a realm with very different rules from the world he had come from. Paytah poured liquid from a metal container he took from the fireplace into a cup and handed it to his nephew. Noticing the questioning expression on Tyee's face, his uncle told him, "Don't worry, you're home now. We will show you around your home."

Tyee had always been the questioning character of the family. Since childhood, he never accepted anything his mind could not grasp. If a realm beyond his sight and touch had helped his ancestors, how could the white man have brought them to this state! While drinking his tea, his mind and heart continued this debate.

Meanwhile, a white wolf entered the tent. Tyee turned to his uncle in horror, but he saw that Paytah was no longer beside him. He crawled back in fear to the farthest point of the tent. When he was younger, his family had many dogs. Over the years, video games, technological toys, and cars had replaced the animals he had raised. Was the bitter feeling of not even remembering the name of the dog he lost, when he was 15, any less than the horror caused by the giant wolf now scrutinizing him in the tent? Where was Paytah? He tried to scream, but no sound came out. The past few seconds felt like hours to Tyee while the white wolf remained unfazed. The non-aggressive wolf finally turned towards the entrance of the tent - its ice-blue eyes still following Tyee. The young man slowly began to understand what his uncle meant by "showing him around the house." As he collected his thoughts, he remembered that the stories he had listened to as a child mentioned a wolf that had saved his tribe from the desert. So, he realized that he should explore his home under the wolf's guidance. He followed the wolf out of the tent. The dawn had broken, and the sun had begun to illuminate the camp. When had the night ended? He couldn't understand. He told himself, "Allow your soul to speak for once." Then he heard the words, "Time is also a measure of the mind. Let your soul speak a little." It was Paytah who was now speaking, but the voice was not coming from outside.

Guided by the wolf, he continued to walk, realizing that it was not just the air that was slowly brightening. They passed through the area that the natives cleaned every morning. The Sioux apologized to Nature first thing in the morning for any trash that could have come from human-made things and then quickly cleaned up the garbage. Tyee saw some pieces of paper among the trash swept by an elderly Sioux. Looking more carefully, he couldn't believe his eyes because these were bills and court summons issued in his name.

The wolf allowed him to observe the swept items for a while. After all, their journey had just begun. They proceeded towards a hill overlooking a large valley. Tyee's heart was racing, perhaps because it was being acknowledged for the first time. Gradually, some faint silhouettes began to become clearer. Tyee could now see the house he was born in. The house, that had seemed enormous to him when he was ten years old, now appeared so small compared to the one he now lived in. Beside it, in order, appeared all the houses they had lived in over the years and, finally, the current one. The houses had grown larger with each move. He thought about how many people happily fit into the house he was born in compared to the house he and his wife could barely fit in now. Moreover, someone had taken out the furniture. The lined-up furniture almost disappeared on the horizon. On the way, he came across the family heirloom chest he had thrown away without looking at what was inside, in order to fit the huge wardrobe. He had difficulty even getting through the door of his new house. The pictures of his father, who he had lost before entering adolescence, were right in front of him as soon as he opened the chest. These were photos of his grandfather and uncles posing on their horses, dressed in traditional attire. Tyee was actually confronting himself for the first time. If there were a divine power, it had taken away his childhood hero, his dear father, at a young age. The resentment in his childhood later turned into anger against this existence.

With the chest reappearing in front of him, he felt the anger rise again. The white wolf also sensed Tyee's anger, suddenly beginning to howl and show its teeth. Tyee had no choice but to calm himself down. Then his father-in-law's house appeared before him. He opened the door and went inside. His wife was talking to her father, but they couldn't see him. She was telling her father how sad she was for Tyee. How he had felt inadequate since losing his job and was crushed under the worry that he couldn't provide the life he had dreamed of for his family. All she wanted was the man she had fallen in love with years ago when they had nothing. She was not after big houses or cars. It was Tyee who wanted these things and blamed his wife for it. The wolf grew restless again. Tyee wanted to escape the house and begged the wolf to take him away.

It was as if they had drawn a circle and returned to Paytah's tent. The wolf came to Paytah's side and laid its head on the old man's lap. Paytah stroked its head as if to say, "You did a good job!" Then he turned to his nephew and said, "Welcome home..." As the young man tried to comprehend his journey outside of Time, his uncle was now preparing to teach him the real purpose of this journey - the concept of *flow*.

44 STORIES FROM THE THIRTY BIRDS

"Tyee, what you have seen since your arrival was meant to help you to face yourself. Because the first condition of being in the *flow* is to be at peace with yourself. To achieve this, you first faced yourself. Now you see the difference between what is important to you in the life you live and what has been dictated to you. It's not your fault. Losing your father at a young age is not your fault either. First of all, make peace with yourself for all these reasons. This is the first condition of flow." Suddenly, Tyee no longer thought about his house, his pickup truck, or his furniture. He had left them all behind. His bills had been swept away long ago, along with much of the trash in his life. He would take pleasure in lying beneath a felt blanket on a straw bed, leaving behind the goose feather duvet and the orthopedic bed whose cost tormented him every night. Paytah said, "Yes, Tyee, this is our second condition for flow: *Doing something our soul loves, not our mind.*"

Then his uncle told the young man that his horizontal journey had ended, and now they would embark on a vertical journey. His uncle grabbed Tyee's hands and lifted him upward. Tyee couldn't open his eyes until the campsite below had become a tiny line. Paytah finally convinced his nephew not to be afraid. Tyee saw a rainbow that seemed within reach if he just extended his hand. Paytah told him he could touch the rainbow as he wished. In fact, all the colors were at his command. Tyee took his favorite color, blue, and drew a sea in the void. Then he took yellow and brought sunlight down upon the sea. Just ahead, he saw musical notes gently swaying in the emptiness. He took 'do' and 'sol' and wrote a song...

He asked his uncle what this magical realm was, fear of the spell breaking evident in his every move. Paytah said, "Tyee, you are in the *flow*, and as long as you are in the flow, you are connected to the divine. The only power that can break this spell is you. As long as your soul is connected to the divine power, its possibilities are at your disposal. Everyone in the flow can use this trust. The only thing that can break this flow is the ambition to possess that trust. This is the third rule of flow."

Thus, Tyee's final lesson was completed, and suddenly he found himself back in Paytah's tent. His uncle continued to stroke the white wolf's head. Tyee wondered how much time had passed. As if reading his mind, his uncle turned to him and said, "This is the fourth and final rule of flow; there is no time for a person in the flow."

Life would never be the same for Tyee. He expressed his desire to stay with his uncle. The old man was delighted with his nephew's decision. He said something to the white wolf in their native language. The wolf looked at the old man with its blue eyes full of affection and left the tent, disappearing into the wilderness. Tyee asked his uncle what he had said to the wolf. Paytah turned to his nephew and said: "Tyee, haven't you understood yet? That wolf was your ego. I told it that you no longer need it. It returned to its wild nature."

"How beautiful it is to settle somewhere every day. How nice it is to flow without getting muddy or freezing."

Mevlâna Celaleddin Rumi

As the Swan finished his story,
the door opened a little wider...

"Unfortunately in this world of ours,
each person views things through a certain medium,
which prevents his seeing them in the same light as others."

The Count of Monte Cristo - Alexandre Dumas

4

THE SEAGULL'S STORY
POINT OF VIEW

C an regretted turning down his wife's offer to drive him to work. He had forgotten that he couldn't trust the weather in Istanbul, as he hadn't been walking for a long time. For a moment, he reminisced about his days at university when he stayed in a student house. He was so agile back then. He had acquired the cars he dreamt of one by one and perhaps added a few centimeters to his waistline with each new automobile. Thanks to a technology company he founded just five years ago, and with some help from the market conditions, he became very wealthy in a short period of time. Now he was making extraordinary efforts to protect this wealth. However, he had no patience for unnecessary activities like sports, hobbies, or vacations in this new life.

The sudden heavy rain ruined his plan to walk along the main street. Angry at himself for carelessly not bringing an umbrella, he decided to take a shortcut through the first side street. He noticed that his new suede jacket was stained due to the rain he couldn't avoid. What other bad encounters would the day bring? Could you believe that the battery of his car, which he had just taken for maintenance, had died, and his day had started this way? He had so much work to do that day... Although he planned to send the company's driver to replace the battery, he was hesitant, since he thought the driver was responsible for the scratches on his car from the day before. He was furious at the thought of paying the re-pairman several times the amount he paid the driver, to fix those scratches. Of course, he couldn't prove the crime, but who else could be responsible besides the driver?

The rain was increasing in intensity, and now not only was his jacket ruined, but water was also filling his moccasin shoes. Can became increasingly angry. He felt a cold coming on as his feet got wet. He was supposed to host a delegation from Japan this week to sign an important agreement. "How could I be so stupid!" He began to berate himself. There was a ten-minute walk left to get to his office; unable to bear the wetness of his feet, he decided to call his workplace. And what did he find! It was unbelievable that so many misfor-tunes could happen at once... His state-of-the-art phone, for which he had paid a fortune, was so wet that he couldn't even unlock it. He tried wiping it with dry spots on his clothes, but to no avail; the screen just wouldn't turn on. Can real-ly thought all misfortunes were finding him as he looked around the street for someone to help him. But since this was a narrow side street, there was no one around except a pa-per-collecting boy coming from the opposite side.

Dilaver was the middle child of a poor family with seven children. Both of his older brothers had succumbed to the merciless conditions of Istanbul, just like their father. As a result of their youthful mistakes, they found themselves in prison at a young age, as was the case in many similar tragic stories. Their elder sister, on the other hand, had managed to become the family's luckiest member by working as an apprentice to a tailor. Dilaver had bought a handcart with the money he borrowed from his sister and used it to col-lect cardboard. Over the past few years, he had gained quite a bit of experience in this field. He could never forget the first day he earned money by selling the paper he collected. With his first earnings, he bought wafers and jelly candies for his siblings. Whenever he thought about the happiest day of his life, he immediately remembered that day. During times of despair, again, he would imagine the smiles of his siblings on that day. As he recalled their joy, he would rediscover the birds dancing with happiness in his heart.

Dilaver was well-liked in his neighborhood because he always had a smile on his face. Meanwhile, a young man in the neighborhood, Mustafa, bought a new phone last week. Nobody would buy his five-year-old phone even if he sold it. He thought he would make Dilaver happy and gave him the worn-out, sticky phone as a gift. Dilaver didn't know what to do with the joy he felt when Mustafa handed him the phone with a smile. He reached out to kiss Mustafa's hand. Mustafa was quite proud that the simple phone he had considered throwing away had made this poor boy so happy. At that moment, Dilaver was in a different world. When he realized the phone could take pictures, his heart began to pound. Just imagine, he could now carry his whole family in his pocket...

Nothing could spoil his mood today, not even the sudden downpour. On top of that, he had found earphones in the trash. Now he was ready with music too. He had his favorite jacket, which he had been wearing on cold days for the past two years, on his back again. The nice thing was that the jacket had a hood. When it rained, he could cover his head without getting wet. He thought about how lucky he was and felt grateful in his heart. There was an abundance in the cart he used to collect paper today; he covered it with a plastic lid so the papers wouldn't get wet either. "How blessed I am today, my phone is playing music too; who could be happier than me?" he thought to himself. He was filled with joy and stopped to look at his siblings' pictures on his phone.

At that moment, Can had taken shelter under a staircase to avoid getting wet, constantly trying to get his phone to work. When he noticed the paper collector he had seen earlier playing with his phone, he approached him immediately. Dilaver was surprised that this well-dressed man was interested in him. In Can's mind, all he wanted was to call his workplace with the phone and escape from this nightmare. The businessman took the phone from Dilaver's hand as if it was his own property. He then turned to Dilaver and said, "I need to use your phone. I'll pay you whatever it costs." As Dilaver replied, "Sure, go ahead, brother," he was also worried about whether he had enough credit on his phone and focused on the potential embarrassment this could cause. Fortunately, the call didn't get cut off while Can was talking. Dilaver felt immense happiness from being able to help, while Can finished his business with the phone and handed the device back to its owner with the demeanor of someone trying to get a dead mouse out of their house. Can had a stack of 100 Lira bills in his pocket. He tried not to show them to Dilaver while searching for a five or 10-lira bill with a hopeful look. However, it was his unlucky day, and he only had 100 Lira bills. He had only talked for about two minutes anyway. He turned to Dilaver and said, "Young man, I'll send my driver later to bring you the money. Don't leave this area!" But Dilaver was already thrilled to have been able to help such an important businessman. That was more than enough for him. "Don't worry, brother. Has humanity died?" he said. He turned his back, leaned the cart against his shoulder, and slowly walked away.

Can watched Dilaver leave and muttered to himself while waiting for his driver, "There are such unfortunate people in this world. How can they possibly be happy?" Meanwhile, Dilaver put his earphones back on, resumed his music, and thought about the man he had just met: "God has given this man such a wonderful life. Who knows how happy he must be?"

"Success is getting what you want;
happiness is wanting what you get."

W. P. Kinsella

And when the Seagull finished his story of the sorrows
of greed, and the joy that comes from contentment
and generosity, the door opened a little wider...

5

THE ROBIN'S STORY
ONENESS

"All for one and one for all."

The Three Musketeers - Alexandre Dumas

I n Dumas' immortal work "The Three Musketeers," there was an unforgettable saying: "One for all, all for one!" This phrase had become a plea for the souls crushed under the banner of individualism underscored by advertisements, especially after the industrial revolution. However, the idea of unity, which stood out as one of the fastest vehicles in humanity's journey, had fallen victim to the confusion of the modern human mind. The only prescription that could solve the crisis of modern humanity was nothing but a sense of Unity.

Let's go back a little... to Anatolia, which has witnessed the birth of many civilizations in the world... The word Anatolia is etymologically derived from the concept of birth. Due to its location as a place where many civilizations have confronted each other throughout history, moments of rupture have frequently occurred in these lands. The 13th century would be one of the turning points for Anatolia in this context. The Turks, while fighting against the Byzantine-controlled

Western Anatolia, were trying to maintain control of Eastern Anatolia, they also faced a reckless Mongol threat from Asia. The collapse of every administration was due to errors in justice, science, and education, which prepared the end for the Seljuk State. A people driven to rebellion by drought, famine, heavy tax burdens, and Mongol oppression, led to the cards being reshuffled for Anatolia. During this uncertain period, a group of wise men who lived by a life philosophy revolving around the importance of Unity emerged, establishing the Anatolian lodge system. In the meantime, the great mystic poet, Yunus Emre, was gifted to us...

It is rumored that the legacy he left for us was hidden away in a 3,000-page notebook. However, this tome fell into the hands of an ignorant person who preferred the moon to the sun, as we see in every era. When this ignorant man named Molla Kasım started reading these texts, he found the ideas on the first 1,000 pages to be objectionable. Molla hastily threw them into the river. The next 1,000 pages were even more harmful, in his view. They deserved to be burned, and Molla did so without delay. If the content of the notebook were known to everyone, darkness would turn into light. How could eyes accustomed to darkness bear this?

Molla reached the last 1,000 pages. As he looked at the text before him, he encountered the verse that would burn him in the fire of regret for the rest of his life.

> "Dervish Yunus, do not say these words crookedly,
> A Molla Kasım will come to pull you to the straight path."

Upon seeing these words written by Yunus 100 years prior, it didn't take long for Kasım to realize his mistake. Of course, it was too late for the 2,000 pages of beauty that had already been mixed with rivers and turned to ash in the air.

But would Yunus, who taught Molla Kasım a lesson from 100 years ago, have said these words in vain? Rumor has it that those that mixed with the water belonged to the fish, and those that mixed with the air belonged to the birds. Now let's listen to a story shared by the Robin, and let it tell us about Unity.

Yunus was in a conversation with his students at the dervish lodge about the Surah of the Bee, An-Nahl. He asked, "Do you know why Allah emulated the bee among so many animals in the holy book?" Then he continued:

"Because the bee is the only creature that has truly integrated unity into its life within nature. Its story is very similar to my own journey. When I came to my teacher Taptuk, he left me alone in a dark cell for days. Just like a larva preparing in a dark cell to turn into a bee. When I came out of the cell, my eyes were opened like a baby seeing the light for the first time. My teacher asked me to purify myself. Just like the first task of a bee emerging from a larva is to clean itself... This was not just an outward cleansing. It was both repentance for my old life and an intention for my new life; the larva had died, and the bee was born. After cleaning itself, the bee immediately cleans the assigned space in the hive; just like the cleanliness of my dervish lodge should be in harmony with my own cleanliness...

My teacher Taptuk assigned me the task of collecting wood for the lodge. Half of my life was spent fulfilling this duty. For 20 years, I collected the most beautiful wood every day, for how could I bring wood that was not worthy of my teacher? I had learned very well that I was one of the dozens of students performing their duties in that lodge. I never questioned my job or the jobs of my fellow students. Just like a worker bee who spends half of its life fulfilling its given duty in the hive in the best possible way. We never feel cold in the lodge, you know, because there is always someone to collect firewood every day. Just like bees huddling together when winter comes. And we never fear, right, because our brothers are always with us. Just like every tired or injured bee that goes outside, the hive is safely taken care of by its siblings. When the time came, I was as sure as my name that my teacher would turn this poor one into a honey-making bee. He expected two things from me; effort and faith. Just like a bee that is aware of its small wings and large body, which are not very suitable for flying. Did you know that a bee can flap its wings 11,400 times a minute? How could a bee fly without much effort? The time had come, and my teacher said to me, "Speak, Yunus!" That day I began to speak and never stopped. Because that day, it was not me who was silent, but the one inside me who started talking. Just like a bee that collects pollen and makes honey on the day it flies...

Every bee is a tiny part of a flawless mechanism that has been working like a perfect clock in a generation of creatures that have never taken a day off for 27 million years. In their 42-day lives, they can produce a twelfth of a teaspoon of honey. In fact, for one kilogram of honey, 40,000 bees must visit 6 million flowers. Fortunately, bees continue to work together as if they were a single body in this difficult task and perform their duties in nature flawlessly. Because for millions of years, no bee has ever worked saying "I." The Surah An-Nahl tells us that the most important feature of a creature in direct contact with divine power is to give justice to the phrase, "One for all, and all for one!" The greatest lesson I learned in the half of my life I spent with Taptuk is this. We are all particles of divine beauty. Alone, we are just one thing, but together, we are everything...

So, shall we respond to the famous saying of Dumas with this phrase from Great Yunus? ***"If we share, we will be full; if we split, we will vanish..."***

And when the story of the Robin was finished,
the door opened a little more.

6

THE DOVE'S STORY
LOYALTY

*"Where there is loyalty,
weapons are of no use."*

Manuscript Found in Accra
- Paulo Coelho

The beliefs of ancient civilizations enlighten our present time through their mythological stories that have
reached us. For instance, we can have the opportunity to
embark on a journey to the world of Hinduism, one of the
cornerstones of Eastern philosophy, through the Vedas. The
Hindu creation philosophy is similar to the stories of all ancient civilizations that nourish from the same source. In the
journey from oneness to plurality, the Creator – God, , first
assigns two opposing forces to establish balance in the world.
Destructive Shiva and protective Vishnu become the two
representatives of the creator Brahma in the world, involv-
ing themselves in the lives of humans. Just like their counterparts in ancient Egypt, Osiris and Set, Ahura Mazda and
Angra Mainyu in Iran, and Yin and Yang in China. Isn't the
basic rule of all civilizations the balance of opposing forces?

Our hero, Narada, is known as the messenger of the gods in the Hindu Vedas. He travels and tells stories accompanied by hymns with his ancient lute called Veena. When Vishnu descends to Earth, Narada always accompanies him and constantly expresses his loyalty. Every word he utters begins with Vishnu's name and ends with it. As his messenger, who could be more devoted to Vishnu than him? Despite being confident in this matter, one day, he can't help but ask Vishnu: "Is there any being in the world who shows more loyalty to you than I do?"

Vishnu invites Narada to join him on a journey; their experience together would determine the answer to his question. And so, our story begins...

Narada and Vishnu descend to Earth and reach a village before nightfall. They become guests of a poor but hospitable villager. When the villager welcomes his guests with Vishnu's name, he has no idea who he is actually hosting. The villager's wife, on the other hand, tries to hide her concern for having just enough dinner for their children behind her smile. Despite being aware of the situation, the villager does not hesitate to serve his guests. When they go to the kitchen, he tells his wife, "Serving a guest is like serving Vishnu," and puts the children's share of food on the plates to feed the guests. The wife, who had prepared a bowl of lemonade for the children earlier, frowns when the guests say they are very thirsty. Noticing this, her husband reminds her not to complain and whispers in her ear that serving a guest is like serving Vishnu. The couple, who give their bed to the guests to sleep, spend the night on the straw. The struggle between the conscience and faith of a father who has given his family's sustenance to the guests keeps him awake, while the excitement of pleasing Vishnu also gives him bittersweet happiness.

When they wake up in the morning, Narada asks the villager about their life. He expects the villager to say that he cannot take care of his children properly due to poverty. However, the villager, instead, simply says that Vishnu always protects him and his family. Thus, Narada asks how many times a day the villager mentions Vishnu's name. The villager replies, "Whenever I remember..." Narada, knowing that he mentions Vishnu in every word he utters, thinks that the loyalty of a villager who remembers him occasionally cannot come close to his own loyalty. He is at ease.

At that moment, Vishnu approaches Narada and gives him a task he is not accustomed to. His mission is to carry a pot filled with oil on his head, climb the hill across from the house, and come back down. Narada, who exerts great effort not to spill even a single drop, accomplishes this task very slowly. Hours have passed, and Narada is drenched in sweat, but as Vishnu's most loyal servant, he also feels great joy in having succeeded in this task. In a short while, with only a few steps remaining, he will reach the peak of the mountain of happiness by receiving praise from Vishnu. However, Vishnu asks an unexpected question:

"My dear Narada, you undertook a very difficult task for me. You covered long distances, carried a pot on your head amidst hardships, and brought it back without spilling a drop. I made you do the work that this villager does in almost a day. So, during this entire journey, how many times did you mention my name?"

At this unexpected question, Narada thinks for a moment. "Not at all..." is all he can say. Indeed, in his effort not to spill the oil, not only did he fail to mention Vishnu's name even once, but it also never crossed his mind to ask for his help. Then Vishnu says:

"In times of difficulty, I am always with you. Those who demonstrate the greatest loyalty to me are those who know I am by their side in those difficult moments."

"My Lord, I will continue on your path,
and I will follow you with truth and loyalty
until my last breath."

William Shakespeare

And when the story of the Dove is complete,
the door opens a little wider...

"If you govern with the power of your virtue (de),
you will be like the North Star.
It just stays in its place while all the other stars go around it."

Confucius

7

THE EAGLE'S STORY
JUSTICE

The insistently ringing phone had spoiled James's Sunday relaxation. Sitting up in bed, he looked at the time and realized it was almost noon. Accustomed to treating himself on Sundays after working six days a week and waking up early every morning, James was also somewhat worried by the phone's incessant ringing. Just when he thought it had stopped, the phone rang again, finally getting him out of bed. On the other end of the line was Michael, his father's neighbor, and close friend. However, his voice was so transmuted that James could hardly recognize him. Michael yelled, "James! Come to us urgently, your father is not well... Please hurry!"

James had lost his mother at a young age, and his father had never remarried after her passing. His father had tried his best to fulfill both parental roles for his son. As soon as James heard the news, he quickly put on some clothes, got into his car, and headed toward his father's house, which was just a few minutes away. This chain of events, which took place in a total of ten minutes, seemed like a slow-motion film in James's eyes. Scenes from his childhood, with his father in them, came before his eyes one by one, reminding him how much he valued him.

His car screeched to a halt in front of the house. Like an arrow, James bolted from the car and reached the door within seconds. Instead of knocking on Michael's door, he was practically pounding on it. When the owner's wife, Jane, opened the door, James saw the woman he had known since his childhood paler than he had ever seen her before. The woman's demeanor increased James's anxiety even more. Upon rushing inside, the young man first saw his father lying on the floor, then Michael, and an unfamiliar man next to him. The stranger was a gray haired, well-dressed man, likely around the same age as his father. Michael quickly introduced the man. Mark was a mutual friend, and the only good news of the day was that he was a doctor.

"James, there's a blockage in your father's airway. We don't have time to get him to the hospital. I need to perform a simple intervention with a tube through his throat. But this could cause permanent damage to his speech..." James felt as if the knife was at his own throat. Unable to utter a word in response to what he had heard, he simply swallowed. However, he realized there was nothing he could do and quickly gave the doctor a nod of approval. Mark, with the demeanor of a player who knew that time was his biggest asset in a life-or-death game, swiftly approached the man lying on the floor. Within a few seconds, he had done what he needed to do. He then bandaged the wound. Shocked by the incident, Michael snapped back to reality when he heard the ambulance's siren. As the paramedics carried James's father into the ambulance on a stretcher, James pleaded with Mark, asking about the chances of his father's recovery. Mark reassured James, as the main issue of breathing difficulty had been resolved.

The three men followed the ambulance in their car. They quickly reached the hospital and began to wait for news from the doctors. This waiting took the young man back to the day he lost his mother in a car accident. The same hospital room, the endless minutes of waiting... He remembered the moment when the doctor came out of the door that swung open like a bar door and the expression on his face, as if it were yesterday. He felt as if the same scene were going to happen again, and his entire defense system collapsed. For a moment, he felt as if he were going to faint. However, this time the news brought by the doctor was accompanied by a smile. When the young man received the good news, he hugged Mark as if he had known him for years. Even the mention of potential speech difficulties by the hospital doctor couldn't overshadow this beautiful moment. James thought about how much he owed Mark and would be grateful to him for the rest of his life.

THE EAGLE DELIVERS A SECOND VERSION

James had made up for the week's exhaustion on Sunday. The increasing noise outside made him feel that the day had progressed significantly. Reluctantly, he checked the time and saw that it was almost noon. He hesitated between getting up and staying in bed, but then he remembered he had to go to work the next day, and he convinced himself that if he continued to sleep, he would have trouble sleeping at night. Out of habit, he reached for the phone on the nightstand, but it was off because he hadn't charged it during the night. When he plugged in the charger and saw the incoming message notifications, he couldn't believe his eyes. There were numerous messages from his father's neighbors. This raised the possibility that something terrible had happened to his father. He called Michael immediately but got no answer. When he finally reached Jane, he learned that his father had had a crisis and that their doctor friend had opened a hole in his father's throat to ensure breathing. Jane told him the name of the hospital and asked the young man to hurry. James was furious. They had tried to cut his father's throat! He rushed to the hospital in a rage. When he reached Michael, he realized that the man beside him was the one Jane had mentioned. Just then, the hospital doctor joined them as well. The doctor told those waiting that there was no life-threatening danger but that the patient would not be able to speak as before due to damage to his vocal cords. James lunged at the man who had caused this harm to his father. How could they do this to the person he valued most in his life! Especially Michael, whom he had never seen any differently from an uncle. How could he have allowed this to happen! Michael tried to explain that Mark had saved his father's life, but James had already made up his mind. It was a great injustice for his father to go through this, and he would remember those responsible until the day he dies, hating them throughout his life.

People sometimes commit injustices because they believe they have been wronged, and they see this as their right. The reason why justice is symbolized by a scale is not only to show that everything is balanced but also to demonstrate that this balance can be disrupted even by a feather. The most important characteristic of justice is that it is contextually subjective, meaning it can appear different from various perspectives. As a matter of fact, this perspective can change depending on whether a person charges their phone on a given day. Having said that, true justice is singular; it merely appears different depending on the mirrors it reflects off of. The quality of the justice one can perceive is directly proportionate to the clarity of that which is reflected in the mirror. That is why life sometimes seems very unjust to some. But those with very clean mirrors are the ones who can see the truth and are the true possessors of justice.

"Being good is easy, what is difficult is being just."

Victor Hugo

And as the story of the Eagle was completed,
the door continued to open...

THE PHEASANT'S STORY
THE ORDER OF UNITY

*"The distance between our hearts is
as short as a daisy's long vision..."*

Gravitational Carnation - Edip Cansever

The coming of the hyacinth to the world is narrated as a tragic story in the Roman poet Ovid's work *Metamorphosis*. Hyacinthus, the young prince of Sparta, is Apollo's closest friend. These two friends who love sports go to play discus throw together, which was popular in ancient Greece. The western wind Zephyrus, shadowing this friendship with jealousy, blows on the disc thrown by Apollo, directing it towards Hyacinthus. The rapidly deviating disc hits the neck of the Spartan. As Hyacinthus falls to the ground, Apollo exclaims before his eyes, "Let me die in your place!" However, Hyacinthus' soul has already begun its journey to the underworld. As a token of this friendship, the gods of Olympus let the hyacinth flower grow from the spot where the bowed Hyacinthus collapsed.

Now let's bring this fragrant flower from the mysterious world of mythology to 15th-century Istanbul. Because our hero is a dervish who lived in this period and gained his fame from the hyacinth. In the most glorious period of the Ottoman Empire, there was a sweet competition between the madrasas - where scholars were educated, and the tekkes - where dervishes were trained, on the path of wisdom. Our hero, Yusuf Sinan, came to Istanbul from his hometown Merzifon for madrasa education and became the favorite of his teachers in a very short time due to his intelligence. Yusuf Sinan was very upset that the knowledge of those in the madrasa was called "kal," a word meaning knowledge and the knowledge of the dervishes was called "hal," meaning behavior knowledge. One day, despite his prejudice against the Sufis, he gave in to his curiosity and gathered the courage to attend the lecture of Çelebi Halife, whom he mockingly called "rice-pilaf Sufi." Çelebi Halife was a Halveti teacher. That day, he relayed a story in his talk that struck Sinan's heart...

The arrows of the Sufis do not resemble the love arrows of Eros; Eros' rumored arrow makes people fall in love with each other, but the arrows of the perfect human make people fall in love with God. Thus, Sinan, who had become the prey while being the hunter, could no longer abandon the tekke. Time went by, and one day Çelebi Halife asked his students to bring flowers they collected from the surroundings. The students engaged in a fierce competition to fulfill their teacher's request. Some made bouquets of roses, which symbolized the heart of a perfect human being in Sufism, while others brought tulips, symbolizing unity. Some dervishes came with carnations representing purity and loyalty, while the number of those who collected narcissus flowers, the flowers of the eyes that always wait for their beloved, was not few.

As the dervishes were occupied with the symbols of the flowers, Sinan appeared with a wilted, bowed hyacinth. The dervishes looked down on this gift, which they interpreted as not showing enough attention to their teacher. Çelebi thanked all the dervishes for their offerings. Then, when he came to Sinan, he asked in a fatherly manner why he had brought a lifeless hyacinth. Sinan spoke of a melody he heard when he listened to nature and recited a verse from the Quran: "The seven heavens, the earth, and all that is within them glorify Him; and there is not a thing but hymns His praise. However, you do not understand their glorification. Truly, He is Forbearing, Most-Forgiving."

Sinan had previously understood and interpreted this verse as the glorification of God by people. However, the verse said "everything," not just people. Now, Sinan could hear the voice of the universe because he had long stopped listening with his ears. It was there that he said, "All the flowers were praising His name. I couldn't bring myself to take any of them. This bowed hyacinth had finished its remembrance and was silent. I brought it, but I know it's not worthy of you..."

The teacher looked at both his humbled disciple and the lifeless, bowed hyacinth. He said to his student, "Oh, Sümbül Sinan! If your neck hadn't been bent and you hadn't been freed from the dominion of your ego, how could you have heard this divine melody..."

In this universe, every being is the instrument of a unique system. Neither too much nor too little... Neither exclusive percussion nor exclusively wind... A divine conductor orchestrates an everlasting melody that plays at every moment. Sümbül Sinan closed his ears, which were listening to the noise of individual instruments, and surrendered his heart to the sound of the chorus.

As the ancient Greek playwright Menander of Athens said: ***"It's time for us to stop tuning into separate instruments and create a symphony together."***

When the story of the Pheasant was completed,
the door opened a little more...

THE HAWK'S STORY
INDEPENDENCE FROM THE WORLD

*"Those who worry about the world have
as many troubles as the world itself."*

Yunus Emre

Like many thinkers who nurture the sprouting of new shoots in the mind, Diderot was also one of the treasures whom people discovered later. Similarly, Diderot's path also involved financial difficulties. In fact, perhaps the financial problems he experienced had never put him through such a tough test as they did on one particular day. Fate had it that his daughter was getting married, and Diderot didn't have a dime left in his pocket. His thoughts couldn't progress as they used to. Aren't the times we feel most vulnerable those in which we feel we aren't enough for our loved ones? Like any mortal, Diderot sought a solution to find a way and a financial resource.

At the very same time, Diderot was editing the work called *Encyclopédie,* which was a contribution to the world. News of this project had reached the ears of the Russian Empress. Great Catherine had made him an irresistible offer. In the end, the Empress symbolically bought Diderot's library, which had a greatness that would delight any intellectual, and then donated it back to him. Thus, the great philosopher would no longer feel financial distress and could focus solely on writing.

The Empress did not stop there! She put Diderot on a salary and paid his wages in advance. The philosopher, who was thus able to marry his daughter in peace, experienced a general relaxation. After the turmoil, Diderot remembered that he had never pampered himself for years and, for the first time, bought himself a magnificent red robe without considering money. In fact, our story was just beginning...

Our hero, wearing his velvet robe for the first time, thought he would do what he came into this world "to do" with even more enthusiasm. He quickly left the bedroom and entered the living room. When he reached the desk where he had written countless articles for years, the enthusiasm he had just felt was replaced by disappointment. The long-suffering desk was full of the marks left by candles.

Diderot constantly used this desk and always wrote here. However, this image, which had never bothered him even a bit until today, was now as glaringly obvious as the small black stones in rice. This desk was no longer acceptable for a royal advisor who had earned the right to wear this robe.

Diderot couldn't write a single word that day. The only thing he could think of was the incompatibility between the desk and the velvet robe. Thankfully, he now had money in his pocket. He immediately bought himself a new walnut veneer desk. The old, long-suffering desk met the fireplace... Now he had a magnificent desk at which he would create masterpieces. As he dipped his pen in ink, he remembered a conversation he had with his friend Russo a month ago. He was about to write the first steps of the great revolution when he noticed the state of the carpet! His eyes looked surprised as if he hadn't been the one who had eaten three meals a day and drank beverages in that room for years. Coffee stains seemed to have embroidered all the shades of brown on the carpet. What philosopher could work under such conditions? With a carpet that matched his robe, he could even change the fate of France!

There's no need to continue the story... Just as our hero was about to complete his third sentence, the entire decoration of the house was renovated in a way that wouldn't compromise the elegance of the velvet robe. However, our philosopher couldn't save France, and the banks were already knocking on his door. For the sake of a robe, not only did the Empress's money go to waste, but the Russian gift of Borsch soup also turned into a debt soup in record time. And finally, our hero was able to put the situation he found himself in into writing. He chose the title of his article, which would later become an inspiration for many psychologists and sociologists, as "Regret for My Old Robe." Perhaps the most striking point of this study was immortalized with the phrase, "I was the master of my old robe, but I became the slave of the new one."

And when the story of the Hawk was finished,
the door opened a little more...

-10-
THE PARTRIDGE'S STORY
SACRIFICE

"Perhaps that's what love is... Passion, devotion...
It's sweet to sacrifice oneself for someone else."

Ivan Sergeyeviç Turgenyev

I n the morning, Dr. Tevfik visited the inpatients at the hospital. As he did every day, he returned to his modest room to compare the reports. He had two more patients to see in the afternoon, but he remembered that there had been an increase in walk-in patients lately. As he sipped his tea, his eyes were caught by the diploma on the wall. There was a photo of him taken 30 years ago. He thought to himself, "I used to have quite a bit of hair." When he lost his first patient, a lock of his long hair had turned white overnight. The sparkle in his bright green eyes had faded over the years. Due to professional duties, he had always eaten little, slept little, and spent more time with his patients than his family. As he took the daily medication for his ulcer, he thought, "If I had to do it all over again, I'd still become a doctor..."

At that moment, the head nurse entered his room with an unusually worried expression. The experienced doctor sensed that something extraordinary was happening. He immediately got up from his seat. It was lunchtime, but of course, he would go to see the incoming patient. The sweet voice of his wife, saying, "This ulcer won't get better like this..." echoed in his ears. But she knew that this voice had never been able to keep him from his work, which he did with love.

As he hurried down the hallway, he didn't even notice Fatma, who was standing in front of the counter. Fatma looked older than the age written on the form she filled out. Her smiling eyes drew a contrasting portrait with the wrinkles on her face. She was confused because she was referred to the "Nuclear Medicine" department, which she was clearly hearing about for the first time. She didn't know exactly what her doctor brother was dealing with, so it was evident that she was struggling to guess what her ailment could be. However, the pain she had felt for a long time was not a good sign, she knew. A few minutes later, Fatma entered the room with the head nurse, accompanied by a woman who must have been her mother. Dr. Tevfik quickly glanced at the reports in the file. Sometimes, when he made a quick, bad diagnosis over the experience of years, he felt very sad. The moment Fatma entered, his instincts had already begun to sound the alarm. No matter how good a doctor he was, he didn't have the power to change the inevitable.

A terrible disease had attacked Fatma's thyroid and had progressed quite a bit. He quickly devised a treatment plan in his head to intervene as soon as possible. While the radioactive iodine, colloquially known as the "atom," was administered, chemotherapy would also have to be started. Dr. Tevfik took Fatma aside and tried to explain the situation to her in a way she could understand. The doctor had a daughter older than Fatma, whom he loved dearly... She never complained about sharing her father with his patients for years. Dr. Tevfik balanced his longing for his daughter with the love he showed his patients. He approached Fatma with the same affection he had for his own daughter. According to the plan, Fatma would come to the hospital within a few days, and the first dose of medication would be given to her. That day, she would stay in the hospital, and the side effects of the medication would be observed. They agreed on this. However, Fatma didn't come to the hospital as scheduled. Dr. Tevfik thought that Fatma might have wanted to see another doctor. After a while, he completely forgot about her.

Two months later, Fatma suddenly reappeared. She had brought with her a girl around her age. Fatma smiled at Dr. Tevfik's surprised look.

"Doctor, my whole family loves you. This is my cousin Azime. I'm not the only one in our family dealing with this issue, Doctor. I brought her to you right away so that we don't delay her treatment..."

Dr. Tevfik looked at her reproachfully since, as far as he could tell, Fatma had not yet started treatment for herself during the two months that had passed. Her illness could have progressed too far by now... With furrowed brows, he asked Fatma:

"My dear, didn't I tell you that we needed to start treatment immediately? Why have you been waiting for two months? I thought you went to another doctor."

Fatma turned to Dr. Tevfik:

"God forbid, Doctor. Would I ever go to another doctor while you're here? My sister had just given birth. My niece was born, and my sister got sick, then we lost her. You saw my mother. How could she take care of the baby? And the baby cried so much, and was so helpless that I felt like her mother when I held her. I don't know if it was because of the love I felt for her, but my milk came in. It must have been fate for me to take care of her, Doctor. But if I had started the medications, I wouldn't have been able to breastfeed her. I couldn't bear it, Doctor. Will you forgive me?"

Dr. Tevfik tried to hide his moistened eyes from Fatma. He had thought that he had spent his life as a doctor, making sacrifices. But the compassion Fatma showed was far greater than all the sacrifices he had made in his life. At that moment, Dostoevsky's famous quote came to his mind: "If you forget yourself for the sake of others, they will always remember you."

And as the story of the partridge came to an end,
the door opened just a little bit wider.

11

THE HUMMINGBIRD'S STORY
FRIENDSHIP

*"What is more delightful than finding someone
in front of whom you can dare to say everything
as if you are talking to yourself? If there were
no one to rejoice as much as you in your good
days, would you enjoy your happiness?
On the other hand, if you didn't have a friend
who would be sadder than you on your dark days,
it would be difficult to bear those days."*

Marcus Tullius Cicero

Long before the white man's discovery, respectful Aboriginal people and kangaroos lived together in Australia. According to Aboriginal mythology, the creator, Biami, personally descended from the sky to create the world. After forming mountains and valleys, he filled rivers with water and created all living things. Everything created by Biami took its place in the magnificent cycle of life in perfect harmony. Finally, Biami created man and woman and returned to his place in the sky to watch his work. On the largest and most beautiful island in the world, Aboriginal people, kangaroos, koalas, dingoes, and hundreds of thousands of different creatures embarked on a journey of millions of years.

One day, a kangaroo was resting by the river with its baby when a koala approached them. The koala seemed very old and was unsteady as it walked. The kangaroo wanted to help the koala, and when it began to talk to the koala, it realized the koala was blind as well. The kangaroo felt sorry for the starving and thirsty koala. It offered its friendship to the koala, left its baby, and took the old koala to fresh eucalyptus trees with the help of its tail. The poor animal was indeed on the verge of death due to hunger and thirst. The kangaroo felt the koala's happiness deep in its heart as it embraced the eucalyptus tree with its arms. But it was also worried about leaving its baby alone. When it went to check on its baby and saw it was safe and asleep, it felt relieved. When it returned to check on the koala, it noticed an Aboriginal hunter slowly approaching the koala. If it didn't do something, its elderly friend would become an easy prey so it decided to risk its own life, unable to leave its friend in such a state. The kangaroo made loud noises to warn the blind koala of the approaching hunter. Although it was fortunate that the koala was able to escape the hunter after hearing the sound, the Kangaroo was now at risk of becoming prey to the hunter. Driven by its maternal instincts, the kangaroo led the hunter away from its baby. After losing the hunter, its only goal was to return to its baby. When it found its baby where it had left it, the kangaroo offered its gratitude to Biami for sparing its baby.

Then, an unexpected event occurred. The koala suddenly disappeared, and Biami's voice was heard. According to the Aboriginal people, Biami not only watched the universe from the sky, but he also tested all created beings by changing his appearance to maintain the order of the universe. This time, he wanted to show the angels accompanying him the friendship of the beings he created in this world. As a result of this incident, he wanted to reward the kangaroo that showed the finest example of friendship without knowing who he was. Biami instructed the kangaroo to break off eucalyptus branches and wrap them around its belly. When the kangaroo did this, the branches suddenly transformed into a fleshy pouch. This pouch, large enough for the small baby to enter, became like a pocket in front of the kangaroo, and it would never be separated from its baby again. The kind-hearted kangaroo was deeply moved, but it couldn't help but think of the other mother kangaroos as well. Biami loved the generous heart of this friend. In its honor, he granted a pouch to all mother kangaroos. From then on, no baby would be lost. When Biami returned to the sky, he told the angels how proud he was of their friends.

"Give me a friend, and I will move the world."

Kemal Sayar

*And as the story of the Hummingbird was completed,
the door opened a little wider.*

12

THE STORK'S STORY
TEMPORARINESS

"Everything is for a day, both that which remembers and that which is remembered."

Life is Short, Don't Neglect to Be Happy
- Marcus Aurelius

Among the greatest commanders in Turkish-Islamic history is Mahmud of Ghazni, who we also recognize as the first ruler with the title of sultan among the Turkish states. Some attribute Mahmud's unstoppable successes to his genius in implementing original strategies, such as using elephants in battle. According to others, scholars like Biruni (whom the sultan called "the most precious treasure of my palace") were behind his great vision. In *The Language of Birds*, the famous Sufi mystic Attar whispers a secret of Mahmud's: a unique piece of information carried on a ring he wore until his death. Our story begins right here...

In those days, when the world was celebrating the first millennium, there were wandering dervishes who embarked on adventures encouraged by the then-new fashion of Sufi schools. These dervishes traveled from town to town like bees, moving from flower to flower. This era presented an opportunity for people who had developed a habit of focusing on worldly needs to meet a group of dervishes who did not conform to familiar ways of life. Our protagonist was one of these dervishes, and he was so unassuming in this world that his name wasn't even known. As we said, these dervishes were a bit different from what we consider normal people. For example, no living being except humans doubt their sustenance. The dervishes, on the other hand, had made it their principle to maintain constant contact with the living world, and there was little room for any doubt in their hearts.

Our dervish, when hungry, would not hesitate to knock on a door and ask for sustenance as a guest of God. When faced with a host who turned him away, he would accept it with grace. During one of his journeys, fate led him to be a guest of a wealthy man. The host, Şâkir Efendi, was both a wise man and the richest man in town. The townspeople always remembered Şâkir with his saying, "I am the one who gives what is given because neither the giver nor the given is mine..." Şâkir never withheld what had been given to him from the guest who had come to his door. In return, the dervish graciously offered the only thing he could: a sweet piece of advice.

"Şâkir Efendi! Allah has granted you such wealth... Always be grateful." The host gave a response the dervish did not expect: "Nothing stays the same. This too shall pass, yâ Hû..."

Years passed, and when the dervish visited the town again, he learned that Şâkir had lost everything in a flood and had started working for another wealthy man. Şâkir was still the same wonderful person, now living in a modest hut instead of the house he had once shared with the dervish. He shared everything he had with the dervish, just as he had done before. Noticing the dervish's sadness at this new situation, Şâkir repeated the same words: "Nothing stays the same. This too shall pass, yâ Hû…"

Over the years, fate continued to present Şâkir with both tragedies and comedies. In another twist, the wealthy man Şâkir had been working for died and left his entire fortune to Şâkir. When the dervish came to visit his friend, he was delighted by the change in Şâkir's circumstances. However, surprisingly, the changes in life did not seem to affect Şâkir at all. The house changed, the clothes changed, and the food changed, but Şâkir remained the same. To satisfy the dervish's curiosity, Şâkir once again said the same words:

"Nothing stays the same. This too shall pass, yâ Hû…"

This was also the last visit during which the dervish saw Şâkir alive. When he returned to the town years later, he found that his friend had, in his own words, "given back the first gift as the last." The dervish had seen Şâkir three times, and as he stood beside his grave. And what was written on Şâkir's tombstone?

"Nothing stays the same. This too shall pass, yâ Hû…"

As a token of loyalty, the dervish wanted to visit his friend, who had gifted him perhaps the most obvious secret of life. Moreover, fate had another lesson for him. On his next visit, he saw that a flood had swept away the cemetery, leaving no trace of Şâkir's grave or tombstone. And finally, the dervish truly understood:

"Nothing stays the same. This too shall pass, yâ Hû…"

Of course, our story doesn't end here. You'll ask what this has to do with Mahmud of Ghazni, won't you?

Life may not be so different for a dervish and a sultan. The dervish has more opportunities to subdue his own ego than the sultan, who has far greater resources at his disposal. On the other hand, the sultan is always at the center of worldly pleasures, successes, and praises, forced to live alone with his poor ego...

Mahmud of Ghazni became the sultan of India in 17 campaigns but had not become the sultan of his own body even after thousands of campaigns when he encountered our dervish. The dervish gave the sultan a ring that would always be with him, a ring he could see at any moment. It was a simple copper ring, seemingly too insignificant for a sultan. But this ring carried a message that made Mahmud the first sultan of all Turkish states:

"Nothing stays the same. This too shall pass, yâ Hû..."

So, it turns out that what made Mahmud of Ghazni was not being the sultan of Ghazni. He was able to become the sultan of the world because he had succeeded in becoming the sultan of himself, and so it was...

And as the story of the Stork came to an end,
the door opened just a little bit wider.

THE OWL STORY
WISDOM

*"There are three things extremely hard: steel,
a diamond, and to know oneself."*

Benjamin Franklin

We, who believe that knowledge is a source of happiness, have been eagerly seeking knowledge since our first day on this earth. A child from Anatolia named Thales, one of our pioneers, introduced what he had learned in Egypt to Ancient Greece, thus laying the foundations of philosophy as we know it today. However, the first person to be called a philosopher was probably his student Pythagoras. Pythagoras, following his teacher's footsteps, received his education from the mystical Osiris Temple, which was the basis of the Alexandria school. The journey from Egypt to Greece was a symbolic representation of the transition from apprenticeship to mastery, and from knowledge to wisdom. When Pythagoras stepped into the Delphi Temple, considered the center of the universe in the ancient world, he opened a window into the world of numbers, looking from the unity of God to the multiplicity of created beings. So much so that Pythagoras defined the entire universe as the construction of 10 special pairs: limited and unlimited, single and double, one and many, right and left, male and female, stillness and movement, straight and curved, light and dark, good and evil, square and rectangle. He said that proportion and harmony accompany this journey from opposition to unity in the numerical world. In a short time, the intellectual circle that gathered around him paved the way for the establishment of one of the world's first philosophy schools.

When the teacher began to teach this unprecedented knowledge, the fascinated students wanted to give him a title. But this title had to be far above what had been heard before. At first, they said, "Only a god can possess so much knowledge." Pythagoras replied, "No, never attribute such exaltation to me." Then the students tried again, saying, "You are at most a prophet!" But Pythagoras rejected this as well. Finally, the students tried their luck with the lofty title "sophos," meaning wise, but out of respect for his teachers in Egypt, Pythagoras politely declined, saying:

"I received wisdom from its true owners. Therefore, I can only be known as someone who loves them."

Thus, Pythagoras added the Greek word "philo" (meaning love) in front of "sophia," creating the title "philosopher," meaning "lover of wisdom or knowledge." The first philosopher of the ancient world, who was also a priest of the sacred temple, proclaimed the brotherhood of reason and the sacred to us thousands of years ago. Perhaps the Delphi Temple would physically disappear under the oppression of time, but the two principles of the temple would continue to live through the philosopher's contemplation.

The first was hidden in the saying "Gnōthi seauton." Which means self-knowledge. This epic phrase was the answer key to the puzzle of existence built on man, the universe, and the creator. The Latin translation, "Nosce te ipsum" or its extended form, "Noverum me, noverum te," means "If I know myself, I know him," or in its Islamic equivalent, "He who knows himself (his soul) knows his Lord." The great Sufi Ibn Arabi explained this truth as follows: Existence reflects some of the Creator's infinite names in their own mirrors. *To know oneself is to reveal the name in that mirror without distorting it and thus to recognize the Creator. In other words, we are all treasures, and the key is hidden within ourselves, in our own being.*

The second principle was revealed in the phrase "Pan metron ariston." This phrase, which would be interpreted in various ways across different languages, essentially conveyed that everything was based on a perfect measure. This principle of Delphi clearly spoke of balance. The roof pointing to the sky was the "one" that Pythagoras called "monad," representing the unity within the plurality. The two descending wings formed the "diad," which had a symbolic representation relating to the masculine god Osiris of Egypt extending to one corner and the feminine goddess Isis to the other, illustrating duality. The child of this duality was Horus, the "triad," representing the balance of the world.

According to Pythagoras, this magnificent system was a weave of numbers that could only be constructed on a foundation of measure. Centuries later, Eastern Sufis would also use the concept of "perfect measure" in describing "kemal," the child of God's beautiful and majestic names in this world. The Islamic counterpart of this principle can be seen in verse 143 of Surah Al-Baqarah: "And thus we have made you a just community that you will be witnesses over the people and the Messenger will be a witness over you."

Just as Prometheus opened the way for humanity by stealing fire from Olympus in Greek mythology, these two principles of the Delphi Temple also paved the way for much of human civilization. After all, darkness is nothing more than the obstruction of light. Though it is worth being mindful of the fact that divine light can never be obstructed. Let us now come to the meaning of the word Delphi. Representing the birth of all this civilization, it is unsurprising that Delphi means "womb of the mother." Pythagoras also incorporated another principle he learned at the Osiris Temple - asserting that, both etymologically and philosophically, everything serves unity of humanity who share the same womb. Therefore, the third and highest principle that emerged was "phil" (love), "-adelphia" (those who share the same womb), or "Philadelphia" – the love of brotherhood.

*"Yesterday I was clever, so I wanted
to change the world. Today I am wise,
so I am changing myself."*

Rumi

*And when the Owl finished the story,
the door opened a little wider..*

-14-
THE PIGEON STORY
SERVICE

"You are what you do,
not what you say you'll do."

Carl Gustav Jung

M uinuddin Chishti, the founder of the Sufi movement with the largest following in the world today, was born in the mid-12th century in a region between Iran, Khorasan, and Afghanistan. Chishti set sail for eastern lands that had never been visited by other Sufis before. The story accepted as the reason for this journey is as follows:

During a circumambulation at the Kaaba with his teacher, Muinuddin was honored with two glad tidings for himself. The first was that he would now be entrusted with teaching, but he could only do this in India. The second tiding fitting his character was that the convent he founded would become the place that fed the most people in a day after Medina. Without questioning this turning point in his life, he set out. He reached Ajmer, a city far away from his home, where he had never set foot and knew nothing about its language, religion, or culture. In a short time, Ajmer embraced this wise man. His beauty and generosity became so famous that not only Muslims but also warring Indian rajas paid him respect. Ajmer became a convent that was the center of the Sufi movement established by this great man, and with Muinuddin Chishti's touch, it welcomed all people, regardless of their religion.

Three hundred years later, in this geography, the Turkish state established by Babur Shah would rule the Indian subcontinent for a long time through its center, the city of Agra. The time of Babur Shah's grandson, Akbar Shah, was the period when the Mughals made the fastest geographical and cultural progress. However, fate was playing an unexpected game for the Mughals. Despite the abundance in victories, the years passed without granting the emperor a male heir. It seemed likely that the Mughals would disintegrate as the ruler had no male child, even though the empire's borders had reached a vast geographical width. As no medicine or treatment worked, a dark cloud settled over Akbar Shah with each passing day. As a last resort, Akbar Shah turned to Selim Chishti, a descendant of Muinuddin Chishti, who lived in a town near Agra and whom he greatly respected. Selim Chishti said:

O Sultan Akbar Shah! I looked at your fate, and unfortunately, Allah did not grant you a child. However, as stated in the verse Al-Imran 189, "The dominion of the heavens and the earth belongs to Allah. Allah has power over all things." In other words, if Allah wills, fate shifts between infinite possibilities; with His power, manifestations are boundless regardless of our limited perception. Akbar Shah felt the warmth of the sun rising faintly at the edge of the dawn darkness in his heart and asked with a warm hope:

O Sheikh, how can I change my fate?

The only condition is service to the Truth. If you're wondering how you will achieve this, you will need to end the service to your ego and start serving the people. Can you do this as a Sultan?

The Sultan recalled the wars he had fought over the years. He had faced countless enemies until now. But for the first time, he was confronted by his 'sultan status' ego, and he had to defeat this relentless enemy for the continuation of the state. When Akbar Shah fell asleep that night, struggling with countless questions in his head, he dreamed of Muinuddin Chishti calling him. Thus, what he needed to do was now clear. But how would he make this journey? He sent his loyal warriors, took off his ostentatious clothes, and finally got rid of his shoes. This barefoot journey from Agra to Ajmer took 17 days. Consider that this sultan had to climb trees, gather plants, and even beg for food on this journey. But throughout the journey, he never complained about his bloodied feet or his tattered clothes.

Upon reaching Ajmer, he went to the tomb of the great man who had called him and paid his respects. He was no longer serving his ego. Now it was time to serve the people. At the Ajmer convent, as narrated for Muinuddin Chishti, thousands of people were fed every day. Akbar Shah had an unprecedented single-piece cauldron made so that enough food for five thousand people could be cooked at once. The Sultan then built many hospices along the road between Agra and Ajmer to make the journey easier for those who came after him. Now he understood what it meant to serve the people. With this sincere service, he unraveled the webs of fate, and soon after, he embraced his son Selim, whom he named after his teacher.

For 800 years, Ajmer has maintained its title as the place where the most food is provided for those in need, after Medina. People from all religions, languages, races, and nations continue to be welcomed at this table, and the cauldron commissioned by Akbar Shah has never failed in its duty to this day...

"The best way to find yourself is to lose yourself in the service of others."

Mahatma Gandhi

When the Pigeon finished its story, the door opened a little more...

-15-
THE FALCON'S STORY
FREEDOM

"Arrogance and obstinacy first make a person see themselves as perfect, and then bring their end."

Tolstoy

I n the 4th century BC, Athens witnessed the encounter between the inflated ego of one of the world's greatest commanders and the annihilated ego of one of the most famous philosophers. King Philip wanted to give his son, who would carry his fame beyond the borders of Macedonia to the remote corners of Asia, the highest education. First, Leonidas and then Aristotle, whom he brought by pouring out his fortunes, trained young Alexander in philosophy, politics, literature, poetry, drama, and science.

Alexander desired to unite the Greek city-states under one rule and end the despotic rule of the Persian King Darius. The young prince had kept Homer's Iliad under his pillow since his childhood. When he closed his eyes, he found himself defeating Hector in the Trojan War, where he saw himself as the legendary hero of the West, Achilles. Neither Leonidas' doctrine based on simple living, frugality, and contentment, nor Aristotle's metaphysical teachings, nor the spiritual satisfaction of uniting all Greek city-states except Sparta in the Corinthian Brotherhood could dam the growing ego of Alexander. Alexander's journey to becoming Alexander the Great began in Anatolia. When he shattered the "Gordian" knot with his sword, he became a messiah-like figure. He entered Egypt without encountering any resistance. He was proclaimed Pharaoh in the ancient city of Memphis at the age of 25. When he was accepted as the son of the god Ammon, not only the people but also, he himself believed he was a god. At that time, he was very angry with Aristotle, who had published his own work on Metaphysics, for sharing the information in the book. This was because Alexander thought he should have been the sole possessor of this information on earth...

Around the same time, in another part of Anatolia, our second hero, Diogenes, was born with a very different fate from Alexander. His father was a counterfeiter accused of forging money in Sinope. The luxury of the family's wealth gave way to misery with the emergence of this event, and the expelled family barely made it to Athens. Unlike Alexander, the pain and poverty he had experienced since childhood led him to the idea that one could live in harmony with nature. When he joined the "Cynic" school, founded by Socrates' pupil Antisthenes and named after the word "dog," his ego had been shattered as if crashing from stone to stone on the streets of Athens.

The Cynics believed that virtue, which they considered the most important feature in life, was the fuel for human happiness, and only those who possessed this fuel could be free. Diogenes astonished the Athenians with the barrel he lived in and the cup he used to drink water, but he also taught lessons to all the statesmen. One day, when he saw a child drinking water from a fountain with his hand, he broke and threw away his cup. For he had learned that every object connecting him to this world was a shackle.

The encounter between Alexander, who believed himself to be a god, and Diogenes, who lived in a barrel, was quite significant. Alexander, influenced by Aristotle, wanted to meet this captivating philosopher of Athens. However, the message he received from the philosopher he summoned was, "I will not go to the feet of the slave of my slave." The "new god" of Athens experienced confusion over this message, which he struggled to characterize as either courage or audacity. The man in the barrel had sent shivers down his spine. With crumbs of metaphysical knowledge he had received from Aristotle, he had a greater enemy than Darius, one of the world's most powerful commanders – his own ego. Alexander, in defiance of his ego, went to Diogenes. He wanted to meet him, for his soul imprisoned within longed to break free from the prison of arrogance. Diogenes explained to Alexander how, with good intentions, he had fallen into a trap as his ego grew larger and how, as he rose, shackles were fastened to his hands and feet. As Alexander grew, so did his captivity. However, Diogenes had freed himself from the bondage of all worldly possessions. He had escaped enslavement to his ego and made it his own captive. Alexander then understood why Diogenes had called him the "slave of his slave." His imprisoned soul made one last effort by, wishing to express gratitude for the lesson - he wanted to shout his thanks to the man in the barrel. He found himself saying, "What do you desire from me, oh great philosopher!" Diogenes was not moved by the question, for he had no worldly desire. "Just don't stand between me and the sun," he said, turning his face away.

Alexander, who set out on a journey to invite humanity to unity as he ends the despotism of the Persian rulers who saw themselves with divine qualities, succumbed to his ego. He became despotic like the Persian rulers he criticized and married Persian princesses, becoming entangled in palace intrigues. The Greek states saw Alexander the Great as a god whom they worshiped out of fear. The Spartans said, "If Alexander wants to be a god, let him be one." At the age of 33, in Mesopotamia, where he declared himself a god, he closed his eyes to this life, succumbing to a high fever. According to Diogenes, Alexander had lived in the world's largest prison. His subjects, who shed crocodile tears when he died, soon shattered the empire.

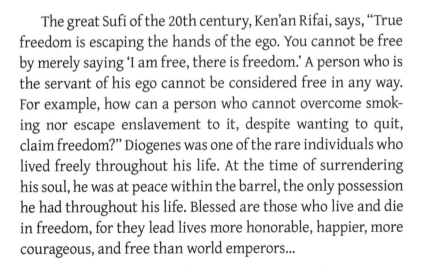

The great Sufi of the 20th century, Ken'an Rifai, says, "True freedom is escaping the hands of the ego. You cannot be free by merely saying 'I am free, there is freedom.' A person who is the servant of his ego cannot be considered free in any way. For example, how can a person who cannot overcome smoking nor escape enslavement to it, despite wanting to quit, claim freedom?" Diogenes was one of the rare individuals who lived freely throughout his life. At the time of surrendering his soul, he was at peace within the barrel, the only possession he had throughout his life. Blessed are those who live and die in freedom, for they lead lives more honorable, happier, more courageous, and free than world emperors...

*"We think we are free. But in our hands
are the invisible chains of our passions,
our bad habits. Invisible handcuffs are
fastened to our wrists."*

Baruch Spinoza

The Falcon completed his story,
and the door opened a little more.

"If you realize that all things change, there is nothing that
you will try to hold on to. If you are not afraid of dying,
there is nothing you cannot achieve."

Lao Tzu

16

THE PEACOCK'S STORY
RELATIVITY

Eastern civilizations are like a delicious pastry made from a dough mixed with morality, baked in a spiritual oven, with a layer of justice spread in between, and decorated with love on top. Let's talk about three great masters who made these delicious pastries in the Eastern world before Christ. They were Buddha, Confucius, and Lao Tzu, each with their own systems of spirituality.

It is said that each of them was given vinegar to taste. Confucius found the vinegar sour, like a world dominated by immoral societies. Buddha found the vinegar bitter, as he envisioned a world full of pain. Lao Tzu, whose name meant "old sage born with white hair from his mother's womb," found the vinegar sweet. His dream world was a combination of harmonious elements he called "Dao."

Dao's world was like a free-flowing river. Those who could not adapt to the flow would be forced to live with the pain inflicted by the stones in the river that represent anxiety, fear of the future, and regret for the past. The river granted freedom to those who flowed harmoniously with it. Lao Tzu once said, "Life is a series of natural and spontaneous changes. Don't resist them; that only creates sorrow."

Now, let's embark on a journey through the story... Our hero, Han, was an unskilled farmer who presented the rice harvested from his field to the palace. Lao Tzu worked in the palace library where he had read every book composed of the unique knowledge of Eastern civilizations. His journeys into the unknowns of the universe, from the highest degree of physics to the mysteries of space, were always accompanied by the books he read. However, the pleasure that came with this wisdom could not match the conversations he occasionally had with an unskilled farmer, Han, during meal times. It seemed as if Han kept a treasure chest of knowledge beyond what could be read, hidden behind his timid gaze. So much so that Lao Tzu began to prefer Han's silence to his own reading.

Han had a white mare. Every morning, she would set off at dawn and arrive at the palace around noon. In their culture, a horse was considered a part of the family. This mare, who had run from the land of wild horses, chose to enter Han's village and allowed the villagers to catch and tame her after several months of causing damage to their gardens and returning home whenever she pleased. One morning, potentially having grown tired of her routine, she appeared in front of Han's house, stamping her hoof on the ground as if to choose her owner. Han named the mare "Yi Ma," meaning "willful horse." Centuries later, this name would be used as "the horse of will" during the Ming Dynasty.

Everyone admired this magnificent creature. In time, the mare was noticed by the palace prince as well. However, the prince's irresistible offers for the mare meant nothing compared to the value Han placed on this family member. Rejecting a fortune that he might not have earned through years of continuous work surprised everyone except his librarian friend, Lao Tzu.

Within a few weeks, an event took place that would add to the villagers' astonishment and prove them right about the man they labeled as "foolish." The ill-tempered horse left the village just as it had arrived one morning! The villagers were dumbfounded when Han did not react as expected, such as hitting his head against the rocks. Although Han, who had lost his only mount, would not be able to go to the palace tomorrow, the day after, or maybe never again, the crowd pitied and somewhat boasted about him. However, when Han told them not to make an assumption about the severity of the situation too soon, he only reinforced the label of foolishness upon himself. He thought about it; the root of the word "fool" came from "ene," which meant "I." In other words, those who could not think of anything other than themselves were real fools. But how could this truth be explained to the crowd? Instead, he could only say, "Please do not make your decision immediately; there is an inner meaning in every matter," amidst the mocking looks of the villagers.

It was not long before Yi Ma returned, and what a return it was! Along with 20 mares! The villagers, unable to believe their eyes, met this unexpected turn of fate with a mixture of envy and admiration. The insincere celebrations meant little to Han. He again objected to the villagers' hasty judgment. Gaining 20 years of wealth in a single night did not make Han as happy as expected. He responded to the crowd's insincere congratulations in the same manner as before: "Please do not make your decision immediately; there is an inner meaning in every matter."

We all know very well that God does not like monotony... Our hero would now be surrounded by new events. Not long after Yi Ma's return with the mares, Han's only son, who took care of all the farm work was injured by Yi Ma's temper, and broke his leg when he fell from the horse. This accident was considered one of the worst misfortunes that could happen to a family who lived by farming. When the villagers heard about this, they visited Han again and offered their lectures, somewhere between advice and mockery. However, Han's submission in every situation did not prove anything to the empty crowd in front of him. The noisy chorus of these people, who could not get enough of being defeated by the wise wrestler, just would not quiet down. Although they did not hear it, Han's answer to those who came and went was the same: "Please do not make your decision immediately; there is an inner meaning in every matter."

Although Han's unquestionable trust and submission to the Creator could not be understood by the villagers, this time, they were soon to learn a new lesson. According to the news, there was a war in the land of China, and mobilization had been declared among the people. Han's son would not be able to be drafted into the war because of his leg injury. As the other villagers sent their children to war with bloody tears, Han's voice echoed in their ears: "Please do not make your decision immediately; there is an inner meaning in every matter..."

This is how it is; making hasty decisions based on appearances cannot lead a person to the right doors. Life is dynamic, and continuity is what matters. The root of the word "decision" is based on the concept of "stopping"...

In Lao Tzu's view, humans prefer the easy rather than the difficult, resting rather than being on the move. Thus, making decisions quickly might seem like a great virtue. However, if the knowledge we think we possess in our own limited capacity is one meter, consider that the diameter of the world is 12,742 kilometers. In a world where the only constant is change, not being open to this is the main source of unhappiness and delusion. Remember... "New beginnings are often disguised as painful endings."

And as the Peacock finished the story,
the great door opened a little more.

"I saw the Lord with the Eye of my Heart. I asked,
'Who are You?' He replied, 'You.'"

Hallâc-ı Mansur

17

THE EAGLE OWL, PUHU'S STORY
PERCEPTION

Yusuf, who knew the streets of Baghdad like the back of his hand, had finally been caught. The streets where he had been pickpocketing since childhood had witnessed what can be likened to "the breaking of the water jug' on its own path." According to the law, he would spend some time in prison, and after appearing before the judge, he would most likely be punished by having a hand cut off.

When the guards took Yusuf to his cell, they did not seem very merciful or generous. However, Yusuf would soon discover that there were congenial inmates in the prison. He anticipated a tough first night, so he tried to surrender himself to the tender arms of sleep immediately. When he opened his eyes again, he could not adapt to where he had woken up for a while. He was so startled by the pitch-black darkness of the cell that he wondered for a second or two if he had gone blind. This made him think, what if he were blind and could not see this ungrateful world? On the one hand, the sound of silence had become an opportunity for Yusuf to listen to his inner world. He now felt a distant melody in his ears. Regular and repetitive... It seemed to echo throughout the cell. He sat up on his bed, which was only a little straw. The sounds were coming from the cell across from Yusuf. He strained his ears a little more. Though unclear, he thought he heard the name of "Allah" being chanted, but it didn't seem to be coming from a person.

Suddenly, lightning seemed to strike the corridor between the cells. The dungeon, which had been as dark as it was a moment ago, was now just as illuminated. With the help of this natural light, Yusuf began to see silhouettes in the cell across from him. He faced a scene that blurred the line between fantasy and reality, a metaphysical panorama. A man was praying in the cell, with shapes resembling moths seemingly holding hands, performing a kind of circumambulation around him. The strange thing was that the sounds had become almost deafening, yet the entire prison remained asleep. Yusuf glanced at the drunken man he shared the cell with but hadn't spoken to since he arrived. He was fast asleep as well. At that moment, the cell walls began to echo the now very distinct repetition of the name "Allah!" Yusuf began to tremble with fear, quickly turning towards his cellmate. He took a couple more steps, but he had no strength left. He collapsed in the middle of the cell.

The cold water poured over him not only woke Yusuf from his sleep but also swiftly brought him back from the realm of dreams to reality. The guard handed him a mush, which he guessed to be made of chickpeas from the smell, and mockingly hinted that the meal he was providing would be the best feast Yusuf would see in this place, while handing him a cold tea. Kays, his cellmate, woke up too. Yusuf seized the opportunity to get acquainted with the man he had been sharing the cell with. He was burning with curiosity, wanting to ask Kays, who he guessed had been in this cell for a long time due to his relaxed demeanor, about the mysterious man in the opposite cell. Kays responded to Yusuf's curiosity with a wrinkled face.

"That man wasn't brought here for ordinary crimes like us. His sin is huge, and an eternal torment awaits him. He is an infidel. The biggest one! A sinner who thinks he is the Truth..."

Astonished, Yusuf tried to understand Kays' terrifying hatred of the prisoner across the room. He wanted to escape from the cell, but he reminded himself that it was impossible. Like a patient suffering from lung pain who falls asleep and forgets about his breathlessness, there was a precious time when prisoners were allowed to go out and mingle in the corridor for about ten minutes. Yusuf waited for that moment like a student planning to skip class. As soon as he got himself out, he caught the attention of one of the guards. The guard must have had some idea or opinion, too, about the prisoner in the enchanting cell across from him... The guard, too, must have experienced what occurred last night, just like Yusuf.

"His name is Hallaj. I do not know his real name. He has been here for years. I have never seen him eat or drink anything. He must be a sorcerer. That's where his name comes from. He says they produce silk from cotton in his homeland. According to what they say, he did some miraculous acts. For example, there was an enormous amount of cotton to be carded by a poor friend of his. Suddenly, this cotton was separated cleanly. Hallaj had done in an instant what his friend had been trying to do all day. From that day on, they call him Hallaj. That sorcerer is a sorcerer... Those bewitched by him flock to the prison every day. They come to see his face... But don't worry, he'll be hanged in two days. Anyway it's none of your business, it's time, go back to your cell..."

Yusuf couldn't sleep a wink. The strange thing was that in two days, they were going to cut his own hand off. Instead of worrying about whether it would be one or both, all he could think about was Hallâj. Time passed, darkness enveloped him again, and what he had been waiting for, happened again. The luminous light he saw the previous night reappeared, and this time it didn't just cover the four sides of the prison cell but infused all the cells of his body as well. Yusuf stood up and turned his head towards Hallâj's cell. He couldn't believe the other prisoners were asleep because all the walls were shouting the name of Allah.

Suddenly, the iron bars opened, and all the obstacles between Yusuf and Hallâj disappeared. Yusuf saw Hallâj for the first time. He was just skin and bones from weakness, but he still looked very energetic. "Welcome, Yusuf from Khorasan," he said. *How* did he know his name? How does this stranger know where he was originally from. Hallâj continued, "Don't worry, Yusuf, I called you here because I have a task for you." Yusuf was caught between feelings of fear and curiosity. But it was clear that Hallâj would explain what was going on, which somewhat relieved him. A magician, a charlatan, a sinner, a madman, or a saint; which one was he? Without even asking the question out loud, Hallâj answered: "All of them, Yusuf, all of them! I know your mind is in turmoil. But let me explain, don't worry... Imagine a white light hitting a prism and being transformed into seven colors, my dear Yusuf. Will you not believe your eyes when you see red, blue, and green? But isn't it an injustice to call red, blue? Oh, my brother Yusuf, all of them are white light to me... I only see that now, but I am different from you. I am red with those who say red, and green with those who say green. That's why I am a magician, a charlatan, a sinner, a madman, and a saint."

Yusuf expressed his curiosity, "But what does it mean to say 'I am the Truth'? I am a simple pickpocket; I don't understand these things..." Hallâj replied, "Dear Yusuf, my teacher Junayd says we made a deal with Allah. Allah gave each of us a right. This world is a journey. We promised to find that right during the journey. I found it and returned the right to Allah. That was my right. I am that right..."

Yusuf didn't know what to say. Seeing Hallaj's state, his heart understood why there were so many people who loved him, but he couldn't understand how one could hate such a person. Hallaj didn't waste any time in providing an answer to this question: "My dear friend, they will tear my body apart, then hang me, burn my body and throw it into the Tigris. I see all of this happening. But you should know that they will do all of this for the sake of Allah. How can I blame them? I love everyone and everything because I only see a single light. We will all play our own games on this great stage. When the bell rings and the play is over, we will return to unity. And peace be upon those who see that unity *before* the bell rings!"

Yusuf knelt down before Hallaj. During all this, the cry of "Allah" had become even stronger. Hallaj pointed to the cell wall with his fingers, and at that moment, the wall of the cell broke into pieces. Turning to Yusuf, he said, "My friend, it's time for you to go." Yusuf was both surprised and happy because Hallaj could escape with him from the prison. However, Hallaj, who could read Yusuf's mind, shook his head from side to side. He wasn't going anywhere. He had written what he had to write with his pen, and the ink had long dried up. Hallaj took off his robe and gave it to Yusuf, saying, "Keep this. Trust that when the time comes, you will understand why I gave it to you. Now go, because this is also your fate.

Until now, you haven't understood what has been given to you in this world. You have now seen the truth, so the path is yours..." Yusuf had actually come to this prison for this new friend, perhaps to find the meaning of life. He had taken what he needed to take here, but instead of being happy to leave the prison, leaving his friend caused him to feel a great pain in his heart. But now he understood better that he was part of a mission. He was to convey his Friend's message to those who could understand it, until the end of his life. He set out on the road, wanting to get away from Baghdad before the unbearable fate that awaited his cherished Friend came to pass. He hid in his old neighborhood for a day and, unlike the people of Baghdad who rushed to witness Hallaj's martyrdom, he followed the Tigris River and headed out of the city. As he tried to get away from the traitorous voices rising behind him, he noticed that the Tigris was flowing very violently for the season. There were boiling spots in some places in the river. Apparently, it was going to overflow and sweep away whatever was in front of it. When Yusuf looked at the waters struggling to reach him, he realized the purpose of the robe. He took off Hallaj's robe and threw it into the crazed river that was pounding against the stones. The fury of the Tigris, which was about to crush Baghdad, found peace with the compassion of the gifted robe. Yusuf's realization came from his new Friend, who reminded him of the following words that he would never forget in his life: "God's mercy covers His wrath." Hallaj was like a reflection of His beauty in this world. If there weren't reflections like Hallaj, the Creator would have discarded this ungrateful world, like low-grade uncarded cotton, long ago...

"They took the intoxicated lover to the gallows,
he first kissed the ladder, then placed his foot..."

Feridüddîn-i Attar – Tezkiretü' l Evliya

When Puhu finished her story,
the door opened even further...

18

THE PELICAN'S STORY
OVERCOMING ARROGANCE

"Pride is my favorite sin."

The Devil's Advocate Movie, 1998

When Homer spoke of the hosts of Olympus, he did not identify that the characteristic features of the gods he had mentioned were actually different from humans; instead, he adorned the stories, which we likened to palace intrigues, with the exaggerated features of mythological heroes and served them at our intellectual tables. After all, these stories were about the Greek gods, facing their own small reflections due to their egos rather than the ontological position between humans and God.

Zeus was one of the most prominent of these mythological characters, and had dominated the sky by defeating the Titans - the only rivals that could be considered equal to him in power. However, he could not show this greatness in front of his wife, Hera. The "first lady" of Olympus was punishing all her rivals who dared to flirt with her husband in unimaginable ways, to the point that Zeus's favorite, Io, whom he had turned into a cow to hide from his wife, had to swim from Olympus to

Alexandria due to a horsefly that was sent to bite her tail. As she passed by, she left the name "Bosphorus," meaning "cow crossing," as a legacy to the apple of Istanbul's eye. Zeus eventually found a solution by creating a fairy girl who would distract his wife with her eloquence. He named this sweet fairy, into whom he breathed the spirit of eloquence, Echo. Whenever Hera had suspicions about her husband, Echo would distract her mind with a long and sweet conversation. However, when Hera realized Zeus's plan, it was inevitable that she would punish Echo. Hera took away the fairy girl's power of speech. With this curse, Echo would no longer be able to do anything but repeat what the person in front of her said.

As time went on, one day, our fairy girl encountered Narcissus, the main hero of the story. Narcissus, or Nars for short, was a hunter. His weapon was not the arrows given to him by his father, the river god Cephissus, but the beauty passed on to him by his mother, the incredibly beautiful Liriope. No one had been able to withstand Nars' deadly weapon. The course of events was the same for poor Echo. The moment she saw Nars, she succumbed to the blow of his beauty and began to follow the hunter unconsciously. When Nars, who noticed he was being followed, asked, "Who's there?" he received a response cursed by Hera: "Who's there?" The poor fairy could only desperately repeat Nars' words. Finally, when Echo revealed herself on a rock, the hunter was consumed by the fire of his pride, which was higher than Mount Olympus. The forest was completely silent. Only the sound of the flowing river could be heard. Then Nars realized that the mournful sound of the river was echoing over the rock where Echo had melted and disappeared.

When the news reached Olympus, Zeus became very angry. He had seen the most horrifying of his creations, arrogance, embodied in flesh and bone... This was the first great sin of civilization, and its punishment should serve as a lesson to all civilizations. If a living being cannot learn to love another living being, it is cursed to fall in love with itself. Zeus sent his daughter, the goddess of justice, Nemesis, to Nars to carry out the punishment. As Nars was by the river where he always hunted, he noticed his own reflection. For the first time, his own beauty had penetrated deep into his bones with the curse of Nemesis. He fell in love with his own reflection, right at the head of the rock where Echo's voice echoed. He spent days without eating or drinking, watching his own reflection. Just as he had drowned in his own pride while alive, his life ended by drowning in the reflection of his own beauty. This tragic mythological story left us a legacy that can still be heard, echoing thousands of years later with an "echo."

Pride has always been considered humanity's greatest problem across all cultures. If there is an end to humanity, it has been said that this end will come at the hands of the arrogant and the self-important. The famous British Nobel Prize-winning poet T.S. Eliot described the impact of pride on humanity as follows:

*"Half the harm that is done in this world
is due to people who want to feel important.
They don't mean to do harm,
but the harm does not interest them."*

And when the story of the Pelican ended,
the door opened a little more...

-19-
THE RAVEN'S STORY
BEING AT THE CENTER

"The answer is hidden in the center of your being. There you know who you are and what you want."

Lao Tsu

Yellowstone, known as one of America's most beautiful national parks, was established in the 1800s. The park, home to hundreds of different species of animals, saw its first human intervention in animal populations in 1930. Elks, known as Canadian deer, were among the park's most popular animals. These beautiful creatures were prey for other residents of the forest, such as jaguars, grizzly bears, and hyenas. However, gray wolves posed the most significant threat to the elks. Humans didn't see this as part of the circle of life and intervened in the ecosystem, thinking their wisdom was superior to ancient knowledge. Without delay, the gray wolves were exterminated. This massacre almost led to the destruction of the park due to a domino effect that lasted for years. Freed from the threat of the wolves, the elks multiplied disproportionately.

As expected, the elks could now graze in the park to their hearts content. Although this abundance did not cause a problem in the ecological balance within the first few years, the greenery where the elks grazed unquestionably began to dwindle in the long run. The native birds of the forest were the first to leave their homes. The real issue emerged when beavers, who utilized willow trees to build small dams in the streams, stopped fulfilling their duties. Streams began to dry up, and the remaining water temperature rose to a level where fish couldn't survive. Forest fires caused by these factors were the icing on the cake.

In 1995, due to the embarrassment humans felt after their misguided intervention in the ecological balance, 14 wolves we reintroduced into the park in attempts to compensate the damage. In just ten years, the wolves brought the elk population to an appropriate level, and forest inhabitants such as birds, beavers, and other creatures were forced to migrate due to the disrupted ecological balance. Simultaneously, eagles, foxes and badgers returned to their homes. Park staff who saw the end of this nearly 200-year-old story said, "None of us realized that when we exterminated those wolves, we were also preparing the parks near destruction. No matter how much we humans think we know, opposing the rules of a nature born millions of years before us is no different than Don Quixote attacking windmills." Therefore, as the most advanced beings with the ability to think in this world, it is essential to understand the perfect system, and act accordingly while staying centered within it...

Let's go back 500 years to the story of a dervish in a distant land who understood what it meant to be centered. Musa Muslihuddin Efendi was in Istanbul Karagümrük, attending his teacher Sümbül Sinan's lecture. As one of the best students in his class, he always attracted attention. The story that placed Musa at the center of the universe took place at Sümbül Sinan's dervish lodge. The teacher asked his students a question:

"What would you do if God gave you the power to control the universe?"

The first student answered, "I would destroy all the murderers in the world." One by one, the other students gave similar answers. Some banished thieves from the world, while others banished infidels. When it was Musa's turn to speak, his answer surprised the other students. Musa said:

"If a good person leaves this world, I pray for another good person to take their place; if a bad person leaves, I pray for another bad person to take their place. Everything is in its proper place, at its center."

Upon this answer, Sumbul Sinan said, "Now, the matter has found its center." After this occurence, Musa took his place in history under the name Merkez Efendi...

"The highest education is not the one that merely provides us with knowledge, but the one that makes our lives harmonious with all existence."

Rabindranath Tagore

When the story of the Raven came to an end, the great door shifted from its place again.

"Give, give until it hurts!"

Mother Teresa

THE FINCH'S STORY
COMPASSION

Michael was on a plane. As he watched the rugged summit of Mount Fuji, he shuddered. He remembered his years of imprisonment in the huge apartment he had built by combining two floors of the famous skyscraper on Madison Avenue in Manhattan, where he had lived for years. He had made it a habit to watch the clouds from his terrace for about 5 minutes before going to his job on Wall Street every morning. Perhaps those were the most enjoyable moments of his life. Now, from thousands of kilometers away, he was looking at the same view, and his mind went back to the wasted years.

People always say that when death comes, the most beautiful moments of one's life appear one after the other like a filmstrip. Scenes filled with money, fame, lust, and possessions tainted the short film that was meant to make one human. It was precisely such thoughts as these that led Michael to cross paths with a Zen master named Daiji in Japan.

Michael had fought great battles with himself for many years to take on a spiritual practice, and to achieve this, he had waged daily battles against his ego. But every defeat had added another medal to his ego's chest. That was until he realized that the more he drank from this sea of unhappiness, the thirstier he became... He thought of "Shoshin," a Zen term meaning: *the beginner's mind.* Since he heard that magical word, reaching that state of mind had become his sole desire.

Before meeting Master Daiji, Michael began training with other students. For months, the Zen monks had him practice Zazen, a practice based solely on sitting and resting the mind. The purpose of Zazen was to attain freedom in existence, both physically and mentally. Michael, however, was preoccupied with the question of how to overcome the mountain of 50,000 thoughts that go through a person's head within 24 hours. He had spent years figuring out how to double the value of his money, how to soothe angry customers, where to get the best cigars, and which wine to buy. Now he had to rewind everything. "How easy it was when everything was complicated; apparently, the real difficulty was in simplicity," he sighed. Then, as time always comes to our rescue, it helped him as well. As the months passed, his mind calmed down, and finally, the day came when he would meet his teacher.

Daiji was quite different from what Michael had envisioned in his mind. In fact, he couldn't help but wonder if this short, stocky man would be the one able to open the gates of the spiritual world.

"Our true nature is beyond our mental experiences," were the first words that fell from the master's mouth when he met his student.

This immediately convinced Michael that he could not possibly hide his thoughts from his master. Daiji asked Michael if he wanted to pursue this path, as the next test would not be easy. The novice, however, was determined to continue his journey. The master then asked his apprentice if there was anything in life that he was never tired of doing.

"Playing chess," Michael replied.

He had started many things in his life, but he had never been able to finish any of them. The only activity that his fickle enthusiasm could not spoil was playing chess. Daiji first had a chessboard brought in, and then he called a Zen monk to his side. The monk had been a servant at the temple for 15 years and had been detached from all worldly matters since the day he was accepted. The teacher told his student that he would play chess with Michael and that whoever lost would have their life taken. The horror on Michael's face was evident, while the monk remained completely unfazed. Michael had been playing chess since he was ten years old, and he was confident in this area. However, for the first time, he was faced with a life-or-death situation, and he had no idea about the skill of his opponent.

The game began, and the cold breath of death paralyzed the seasoned player like a viper's venomous bite on its prey. Every thoughtless move was crushed under the indifferent moves of his opponent. As the deadly finale became inevitable, Michael realized that all his anxiety-ridden thoughts were starting to vanish like balloons popping in a room filled with needles. The flow of the game had suddenly changed. Michael was now winning. But as the game progressed, a new thought entered his mind. His opponent had been so successful in his journey that he had no remaining desires related to himself; he was extremely innocent. Suddenly, Michael's entire body was filled with compassion. If he won this game, the world would lose such innocence. His own life was so insignificant compared to this beauty. He deliberately made wrong moves and allowed the monk to win.

From the day he entered the room, Michael knew that he would have to give his life to this path, but he never imagined that surrender would taste so sweet. Voltaire said, "Man bends before intelligence but kneels before compassion." Michael now felt this quote in every cell of his body. Daiji smiled, declared that this game had no loser, and explained the true meaning of the events to his student. The Zen monk was blind to the factors of this world, so the threat of death did not affect his motivation in any way. However, for Michael, death was a significant threat. Yet, as the possibility of death approached, his thoughts gradually diminished. The master said:

"Death came so close that there was no room left for your thoughts to move. Then your mind detached from all kinds of thoughts. After that, love, the true essence of our creation, infiltrated your body and introduced itself as compassion. You reached a mind that could sacrifice its own self for someone else, and you decided to lose. Thus, you won..."

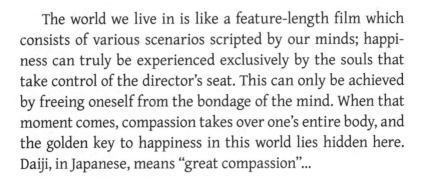

The world we live in is like a feature-length film which consists of various scenarios scripted by our minds; happiness can truly be experienced exclusively by the souls that take control of the director's seat. This can only be achieved by freeing oneself from the bondage of the mind. When that moment comes, compassion takes over one's entire body, and the golden key to happiness in this world lies hidden here. Daiji, in Japanese, means "great compassion"...

*"The meaning of compassion is to be passionate
about everything. Not just between two people...
For all people, for all things on earth, for animals,
trees, everything the earth holds..."*

Jiddu Krishnamurti

*When the Finch's story was finished,
the door had opened a little more...*

-21-
THE CANARY'S STORY
HUMILITY

"Humility is not thinking less of yourself,
but thinking of yourself less."

C. S. Lewis

This story is about how one of history's greatest commanders and wealthiest kings encountered humility.
The Hanging Gardens of Babylon, one of the seven wonders of
the ancient world, were said by Greek and Roman historians
to span an area of 20 stadia, with magnificent beauty. Built
by King Nebuchadnezzar in the 5th century BC as a token
of his love for Queen Amytis, these gardens were specially
designed to prevent the queen from missing her homeland,
Media. The walls surrounding the gardens contained castles
and temples with giant statues made of pure gold. The Tower
of Babel, the tallest tower the world had ever seen, was built
to reach heaven and was dedicated to the god Marduk.

This masterpiece was established in the lands of Mesopotamia, between the Euphrates and Tigris rivers, which

were considered the most fertile lands in the world and were described as earthly reflections of two of the four rivers of paradise. As a result, over the centuries this region had witnessed a cycle of ancient cities rising and falling, both historically and spiritually.

As Babylon, which meant "Gate of the Gods," grew under Nebuchadnezzar's rule, he felt his own greatness increase. He was an undefeated commander, an artist, and a king whose wealth grew every day. However, as the king's grandeur grew, so did the darkness that enveloped those magnificent lands. As if it were a law of nature, as the darkness grew, a light that would balance it turned towards Babylon. According to legend, a prophecy foretold that a leader who would bring about Babylon's end would come from the Israelites. Upon the kings order on a specific day, all newborns were to be killed. However, one family managed to escape this massacre and desperately hid their child in a cave. This child, raised by two lions—one male and one female—was none other than the Prophet Daniel.

When the tyrant king conquered Jerusalem, he destroyed Solomon's temple, showing great disrespect to the sanctity of the Israelites. He enslaved most of the people and presented them as gifts to his commanders. He brought important officials, including Daniel, to serve him in his palace in Babylon.

Nebuchadnezzar placed great importance on dreams. He had his dreams interpreted by his own soothsayers. One evening, he had a dream that greatly affected him, and he was certain it concerned his future. More than ever, he was eager to have the correct interpretation of this dream than with any of his previous dreams. He took this matter so seriously that he thought the person who could accomplish this task should have the ability to know the details of his dream without him telling it. When the soothsayers said such a thing was impossible, the king threatened to kill them. Upon hearing this news, the Prophet Daniel prayed to God to save innocent lives. God, then revealed Nebuchadnezzar's dream to Daniel and gave him the means to interpret it.

In the dream, an astonishing statue was depicted. Its head, made of gold, rose majestically towards the sky. After a while, a mere stone from an unseen source struck the statue and toppled it over. While explaining the dream, Daniel said that the statue symbolized the king and that if he did not maintain his wealthy reign with justice and humility, it would be destroyed by a piece of earth. Nebuchadnezzar was greatly impressed by this interpretation and appointed the Prophet Daniel to be his advisor.

In a short time, however, the king was again blinded by the world's riches and began to forget this dream. Although the Prophet Daniel tried to invite the king to humility, the enchantment of his growing worldly love had already intoxicated him. Subsequently, the king had a second dream. In this dream, there was a tree rising to great heights. But an angel shook all its leaves, fruits, and branches off. In a short time, the tree remained as only a trunk, and the angel declared seven times it would remain this way.

The Prophet Daniel interpreted the second dream, which foretold that the king would receive retribution for falling into the trap of pride again, despite the previous warning. The king would soon lose his mental faculties and flee the palace, living amongst the animals in the forest for seven months. The fulfillment of the dream did not take long...

When Nebuchadnezzar regained his former faculties at the end of these seven months, he had become a very different person. The king could have been the most powerful and wealthiest ruler of his time, but he had learned through great difficulty, that true virtue was humility in the midst of this wealth...

This story was like a continuation of the first lesson experienced by mankind. The devil, created from fire, was commanded to prostrate before Adam who was created from earth – this illustrates the need for pride to bow before humanity. Earth always remained underfoot and continued to serve those who stepped on it.

"He who does not think himself great
is greater than he imagines."

Wolfgang von Goethe

When the Canary finished the story,
the door had opened a little more...

THE HUMA BIRD'S STORY
WEALTH

"Riches serve a wise man, but rule a fool."

Seneca

Being as rich as Karun" is a phrase that lights up the eyes of those who say it and brightens the imaginations of those who listen. But would those who know Karun's story really want such wealth, I wonder?

The insatiable ambition of humans for worldly possessions has always been a persisting weakness. Despite the fact that, Alchemy, which traces back to the first human, was originally bestowed upon humans as a special branch of chemistry to obtain valuable metals from worthless ones, it eventually was to be used in service of their insatiable ambition. According to legend, an element not found on Earth was given as a gift. Known as red sulfur, this element enabled the transformation of a seemingly worthless metal like copper into gold. When God commanded Prophet Moses to write the Torah in gold, this knowledge was also granted.

Karun, the cousin of Moses, acknowledged his prophethood and tried his best to follow his path. However, Karun was so poor that he couldn't even perform his prayers due to starvation. Moses, taking pity on him, taught him the knowledge of alchemy. In a short time, Karun accumulated an immense fortune by turning the simple metals in his possession into gold. A new path was now laid out for Karun. While some of the people continued their loyalty to Moses, others flocked around Karun, who had suddenly become wealthy.

Spending most of his time on alchemy, Karun's prayers quickly turned into hastily performed rituals. Moses was concerned but took no action without a command from God. When it was time for Karun to give his alms, the weight of his gold-engorged ego was too much to bear. He sought to humiliate Moses in front of the people by refusing to give alms and resorting to slander. He bribed a woman to accuse Moses of adultery. However, God foiled this plan. Moses was saddened by Karun, who did not share the worldly riches he had amassed with his brothers, having used the alchemical knowledge that Moses had taught him. God sent Gabriel to help his prophet. Gabriel placed the Earth under the command of Moses and told him that he could punish Karun however he wished.

Moses went to his cousin, who did not even attempt to rise from his golden throne. Moses struck the ground once with his staff and commanded, "Swallow!" The Earth first swallowed the throne. When the command "swallow" was given again, Karun was buried in the ground up to his waist. He begged for forgiveness, but Moses gave the third "swallow" command. The Earth swallowed Karun and all the people who followed him. Moses knew that there were people who envied Karun's wealth even though they did not follow him. He gave the command "swallow" one last time, and all the accumulated wealth merged with the Earth. According to the legend,

Karun would continue his journey downward into the Earth until the Day of Judgment.

As for the secret of the red sulfur, alchemy was indeed a knowledge granted to humanity by God. People believed that copper was transformed into gold through alchemy, but in reality, the red sulfur did not turn copper into gold. As a matter of fact, gold could be extracted once the copper was purified; it was merely a metal that emerged when its copper covering was cleansed. Since it was rare, its value increased in the eyes of the people. In reality, the true alchemist cleansed the person in front of him of all the worthless, ego-like metal to encourage the revelation of their valuable spirit. Those who did not understand the philosophy of this knowledge, however, became accustomed to seeing their worthless metals - their egos, as valuable. Instead of allowing the alchemist beside him to reveal his spirit, Karun played the alchemist himself and polished his ego more and more. Eventually, his ego blinded him so much and weighed so heavy, that being swallowed into the Earth became inevitable. The true wealth was not in the riches Karun built to satisfy his insatiable needs but in the *poverty* Moses built on his *lack* of needs.

*"The poorest man in the world is
the one who has nothing but money."*

Arthur Schopenhauer

*When the Huma Bird finished its story,
the door rattled again and opened a little wider.*

23

THE SWALLOW'S STORY STRUGGLE

"Kites rise highest against the wind, not with it."

Winston Churchill

Sushi is a type of food discovered by the Chinese in the 2nd century, but over time it has been adapted by the Japanese to their own cuisine. The Chinese used the fermenting properties of rice to store raw fish for a long time. Thus, for the first time in a country's cuisine, the partnership of fish and rice began. However, this partnership ended when the rice used to store the fish for long periods was disposed without being consumed. The Japanese took this idea from their neighbors and began eating rice with fish. In the 17th century, a chef in Tokyo made sushi to be consumed immediately after preparation. In other words, sushi became "fast food" as we know it today. By fermenting with vinegar instead of rice, Matsumoto played a crucial role in the final form of sushi. As a result, a dish was created that, unlike tradition, used fresh fish prepared and consumed quickly.

Sushi, deserving to be the national dish of Japan, quickly captivated the entire nation. This rapidly increased the demand for fresh fish. Being an island nation, fish were already being caught in abundance. However, the growing demand day by day pushed the fishermen to new water basins where they could find more fish. Over time, the further the fishermen went, the longer it took them to return. The lengthening of the process, from taking the fish out of the sea to placing it on the plate changed the quality of the dish, and as a result, the Japanese people began to miss that famous fresh taste they were used to. Thus, interest in sushi suddenly decreased.

To solve this problem, fishermen started to add water tanks to their boats so that the fish could stay alive for a long time. This way, even if the fishermen's return to shore took a few days, the fish would continue their lives in the water tanks, preserving their freshness. However, this plan didn't work, and fresh sushi made from the fish brought in the water tanks didn't attract the expected interest. This is because when the caught fish were taken on board, they left behind not only their homes in the ocean but also their hopes and desires to live. Therefore, when they were trapped in the water tank, they had no motivation left to struggle for life. Even the skillful hands of the mastercooks were insufficient to flavor the fish that reached the tables in this way.

Finally, a Japanese fisherman who could transfer his life experiences to his kitchen put his ingenious idea into practice and released a small shark into the tank. The water tanks were designed for the fish to swim in. Before the shark's visit, the fish in the tank preferred to remain idle in a purposeless manner, but the new situation broke the vicious cycle created in this artificial habitat. Now a new factor had entered the scene, triggering the fish's survival instincts. During the journey in the water tank, many of the fish managed to survive by struggling and reached the hands of sushi masters, preserving their freshness. Thus, the problem of losing the freshness and taste of the caught fish was solved.

Indeed, our life journey is much more complicated than a fish's journey from the ocean to the table. However, without the small sharks that keep us alive in our struggle for life, it is not a far-fetched possibility that we become like the living dead, trapped in a water tank...

As Bernard Shaw emphasized, *"If there are no difficulties on the path you walk, that path will lead you nowhere."*

When the story of the Swallow bird was over,
the great door opened a little more.

"We are what we think.
All that we are arises with our thoughts.
With our thoughts, we create the world..."

Gautama Buddha

24

THE KITE'S STORY
SURRENDER

There once was a prince, who lived 2600 years ago, imprisoned in his own "matrix" called the palace. In his 29 years of life in the palace, he had never encountered a single death, a sick person, or an elderly person. However, this palace, surrounded entirely by blessings, tormented his soul to the point where he felt like he was fighting an eagle which was tearing out his liver. Our prince eventually left the palace, giving in to his emotions and setting out on a journey of discovery.

On the first day, he stepped out into the world. He encountered death, illness, and old age, things his people witnessed daily, but he was meeting for the first time. It was natural for the prince to be astonished by these revelations. However, he considered these new things as blessings, unlike the ones he was accustomed to in the palace. He was eager... He chose to explore, to know, to see. He awoke so profoundly from his slumber that he was thenceforth called "Buddha," meaning "the awakened one."

Our story's hero is a young woman named Kisa Gotami, who lived during the same period as the Buddha. Gotami was married to the only son of a wealthy family in the town. When this only child's first baby was to be born, the entire town joined the celebration.

The birth of this male child brought great joy to the family. However, the baby's departure was as swift as his arrival. Gotami witnessed the motherly affection she had tasted for the first time fall and shatter into a blind pit. When she took her baby's lifeless body and started going door to door, the last remnants of her sanity were swept away by the blind hope of a divine power that could bring her child back to life. If Mephistopheles from Faust had been there, a single signature would have sufficed for a deal. But one of the doors offered her fresh hope. After all, the "awakened one" was there, and surely, he was the one who could solve this complex equation.

Having encountered death on his journey of discovery and experiencing it so intensely that he was reborn as a human, Buddha was the only goal Gotami wanted to reach. Buddha, on the other hand, now spent the traces of abundance and prosperity from his years as a prince, sitting under a Banyan tree. This seemingly frail sage, contrary to expectations, was internally strong as a wrestler. When Gotami met Buddha, she couldn't even be bothered by the paradox of the most exalted being in Nepal and this weak man before her. All she wanted was for her son to come back to life.

Buddha told the young woman what she wanted to hear. Yes, there was a solution to bring the child back to life. And all it took was her finding a simple mustard seed, which was undoubtedly to be found in every home of the town. But Buddha had one more condition. The house from which Gotami would ask for the mustard seed must not have experienced death.

Buddha had learned about the world's two most genuine concepts, birth and death, under the very Banyan tree, where he now sat in Gotami's shadow after leaving his deceitful way of life of 29 years, and yet having never seen death. Now it was Gotami's turn to learn. She left Buddha and set out to do what he had told her. She headed to the first house she came across and knocked on the door quickly. Gotami eagerly asked the homeowner for a mustard seed, and the homeowner immediately brought one. However, when it came to the second criterion, the homeowner helplessly revealed that their mother had died the previous year. Though the house had a mustard seed, it had witnessed death.

Gotami then turned to another nearby place, hoping to find a mustard seed in a house that had not witnessed death to bring to Buddha. But in that house, although there was a mustard seed, the woman who opened the door said she had miscarried five years ago. When Gotami reached the back of the house, she learned that the man's wife had died in a flood years ago. Gotami had promptly searched the entire town for a mustard seed, and the famous saying echoed in her head: "The living are few, the dead are many..."

Gotami spent long days going to every place in the area, tirelessly knocking on every door she encountered. She found a mustard seed in every house, but she saw that there wasn't a single house that hadn't witnessed death. She couldn't maintain her hope and noticed that her strength to continue searching was dwindling. Eventually, as time continued to flow, she came closer and closer to giving up. When she realized she had reached the end of the road, she felt a strange sense of coolness inside her. It was as if a hole had opened at the bottom of the pool of despair she was swimming in, and the pool began to empty. So much so that the death stories of the people whose doors she knocked on for a mustard seed allowed her to share their pain. She had divided her own pain amongst these stories, digesting her pain step by step at each door. And finally, she had accepted the reality of death, the sharpest cog of the magnificent mechanism.

When Gotami returned to Buddha, she had no mustard seed in her hand. The smile on the face of the awakened one swept away every shadow in Gotami's heart into the dustbin of awareness, emptying and wiping it away completely. Gotami's love for her baby was no longer under the dark shadow of death, the only certainty of this world.

As it was said in Richard Bach's unforgettable work, *Jonathan Livingston Seagull*, **what the caterpillar called the end of the world, the master butterfly called it a beginning...**

When the Kite's story ended,
the door opened still further...

"We must learn to live together
as brothers or perish together as fools."

Martin Luther King, Jr.

-25-
THE CRANE'S STORY
UNITY

In the mid-19th century, a severe famine loomed in northern Europe. Ireland was one of the countries most affected by this threat. Potatoes, one of the main food sources for the people, were almost entirely depleted in the country due to an unexpected epidemic. In the following years, Ireland, unable to solve this problem, particularly suffered through 1847, known as "Black 47", when the famine was at its worst. With the approach of winter, Dublin was ravaged by hunger, and the surrounding villages struggled to survive on their own.

Leighlinbridge, a classic Irish village composed of winding streets and ancient ruins, was sharing the same bitter fate as all the villages near Dublin. Most of the villagers were farmers, so they tried to put whatever they could grow on their tables one evening. They consumed the scarce produce they had, a little fearfully and a little shamefully, silently behind thick curtains. Around this time, the legendary story of a stranger who made soup from a magical stone began to circulate among the people. According to the rumor, a man came to the villages with a pot in hand, making delicious soups using only water and a magic stone.

One morning, this mysterious stranger appeared on the quiet streets of Leighlinbridge. The news slowly began to spread amongst the villagers who had locked themselves in their homes. Succumbing to their curiosity, one by one they started to observe the stranger from a distance, to witness the fire he lit in the village square. The stranger's strength was evident even from afar as he carried a pot almost as big as himself, as if it were a toy. After lighting the fire and placing the pot on it, with every bit of water the stranger carried from the village fountain to the pot, the curiosity of the villagers grew exponentially.

Meanwhile, villagers began to crowd the square. They all wanted to see the famous stone that could turn water into a unique soup. The stranger started stirring the soup with a large ladle. Yes, there was a green stone attached beneath the ladle! Now, the villagers stared at this stone about which they were most curious. The stranger brought the ladle to his lips for the first time and made a sound indicating satisfaction with the taste of the soup. "I wonder what it would be like if we added some pumpkin?" he asked aloud. One of the villagers gathered the courage to approach the stranger. Although it was obvious that his purpose was to see the green stone, he said he had some pumpkin and wanted to add it to the soup. In return, he expected the stranger to reveal the secret of the soup.

As the stranger put the pumpkins he received from the villager into the soup, he pointed out the birds flying south due to the approaching winter. He continued:

"Look at the birds! Do you know why they fly in a V-shaped formation? Each bird's wing flap creates lift for the bird immediately behind it. With this method, the entire flock achieves about twice the flight distance as each bird flying alone."

While the villagers were thinking about the relationship between the stranger's words and the magic stone, another villager came forward with some onions. They could smell delicious aromas and thought they might not get the desired taste without onions. After thanking the villager who brought the onions, the stranger continued his speech:

"When a bird leaves the V-shaped formation, it suddenly feels the difficulty of trying to go alone and quickly rejoins the formation to benefit from the lift of the bird in front."

During the conversation, another villager added some eggplant to the pot. The stranger, however, continued his speech about the migrating birds, undisturbed:

"When the leading bird gets tired, it moves back in the formation without breaking the line, signaling the bird behind to take its place."

At this point, the village butcher, unable to resist the aroma of the soup, brought some previously hidden pieces of meat and threw them into the pot. The stranger, however, continued his speech:

"Birds make noise from behind to encourage those in front to maintain their speed..."

As the villagers listened to this intriguing conversation, they continued to bring provisions from their homes and added them to the pot. The soup was almost ready now. However, no one had yet learned the secret of the stone.

"Lastly, and I think this is the most important, when a bird gets sick or injured, two other birds accompany it to provide help and protection. They stay with the bird until it can fly again or until it dies, and only then do they return to the flock."

The soup was now ready, and all the villagers approached the pot, reveling in the pleasure of witnessing this miraculous event. But they knew that when the stranger took the stone and left for another village, the feast would come to an end. The stranger removed the green stone from the string tied to the ladle and threw it into the stream flowing through the village center. Turning to the astonished villagers, he said:

"The power that brought this delicious soup to this state wasn't a magical stone, but the strength born from your unity. Be like the birds, so you can draw strength from each other, cover each other's shortcomings, and warn each other when one goes astray. Most importantly, never leave anyone behind. This soup that filled all our stomachs tonight came into being not through a stone, but through your togetherness..."

"The strength of the pack is the wolf,
and the strength of the wolf is the pack."

Rudyard Kipling

And as the Crane finished speaking,
the door, yet again, continued to open.

-26-
THE FALCON'S STORY
MERIT

"A deserving and tested slave is better than
a thousand sons. This saying is meant in this sense:
An obedient servant is better than 300 sons.
A son wishes for his father's death, while the other
desires his master's elevation."

Siyasetnâme Nizâmülmülk

Salih Usta was nearing the completion of almost 40 years in the factory that he had entered as an apprentice during his adolescence. Over the years, he had passed through the lathe of every department in the factory. His hard work throughout his career helped Salih Usta, who was self-taught, never to feel inferior to his educated counterparts. However, he now thought he was nearing the end of the road and was looking for an opportunity to pass on the many years of experience he had, to the younger generations.

In recent years, the company had begun to prioritize hiring university graduates in an effort to rejuvenate itself. These young employees, who were just starting their working lives, had an excessive amount of self-confidence. Although

Salih Usta attributed this to the inexperience of the youth, he did not want them to go through this period with its potential misfortunes. He even had to warn Barış a few times because of his occasionally overbearing and boastful behavior - he had made a habit of frequently mentioning his school.

Salih Usta would have conversations with his colleagues during lunch breaks once or twice a week. They would discuss ancient stories, and he would try to relate these stories with his work experiences, as much as he could. One day, during dessert at lunch, a story was told at the table, where the young employees were also listening. The story concluded by making the point that accidents were caused by inexperienced drivers, rather than experienced ones, who might think they were beyond even having accidents. Barış, who must have taken this personally, interjected, "A good driver is one who uses his car as if it were a part of his body. Whoever feels this way will never have an accident." He also added, "It's the same with work. Some people become masters in ten years, while others can achieve it in just ten days." Barış's confidence was total, as his work had become almost an extension of his being, in a short time. Salih Usta politely told Barış that no one should be too sure of his or her merit. He began to talk about the hero of the story he wanted to tell.

Salih Usta was going to talk about one of the most distinguished figures in the history of Sufism. An 11th-century scholar who grew up in the "House of Wisdom" in Baghdad, the largest knowledge center of the ancient world. A teacher who illuminated thousands of students from his own school, even after his death... Abdülkādir of Gîlân. Abdülkādir, the founder of the Qadiriyya order, was known as the teacher of teachers in all schools of Sufism. Just as a delicious meal is cooked slowly over low heat, the students of these schools were also subject to a curriculum based on patience in their lodges.

Hasan was a disciple who had been trying to fulfill his duty of making halva in Abdülkādir's kitchen for a long time. He had made great progress since he set out on this spiritual path. However, despite the years that had passed, his teacher kept him working in the kitchen. Hasan's potential was high. He absorbed all the teachings, such as jurisprudence, hadith, and theology, like a sponge. He couldn't help but compare himself to other disciples from time to time. For example, while some newcomers had started to give talks, Hasan felt he was standing still, and day by day, he felt as if he was losing himself in the vortex of the halva he was stirring.

One morning, Master Abdülkādir came down to the kitchen and approached Hasan. A prince in India, who was his own student, had died, and he had no son. Therefore, the kingdom requested help from Abdülkādir. The master turned to Hasan and offered him the sultanate of Gujarat. After all, Hasan had complete confidence in himself. Hasan accepted the task with great joy. However, his teacher had one condition: when the time came, Hasan would give half of everything he gained as a ruler to his teacher.

Without hesitation, Hasan accepted this agreement. He lived happily, trading the spiritual education he had received over the years by the halva pot, for treasures, palaces, and concubines. The years had also granted him a male child. Perhaps he would die one day, but his name would be written in history, in golden letters, as a king, and his lineage would continue.

Years later, one day, he learned that his teacher had come to visit him with a caravan arriving from Baghdad. Hasan welcomed his teacher with great care. He knew it was time to settle accounts, but he had amassed such a great fortune that he had no fear of giving half of it to his teacher. However, an unexpected proposal came from his teacher. After Hasan became the Raja, a male child was born. Therefore, according to the agreement, he also had to be shared. When Hasan asked how this would be done, Abdülkādir suggested that the child should be cut in half. The heir was brought before the teacher, and when Abdülkādir drew his sword, Hasan, to protect his son, pulled the dagger from his belt and lunged to stab his teacher's heart.

Within a split second, Hasan found himself back in the kitchen where he had spent years, plunging the wooden spoon he had been holding a few seconds ago into the halva instead of the dagger. Stunned, he inhaled the smell of the hot oil soaked into his much larger gown that replaced the kaftan he had been wearing moments ago, which now felt like years. His teacher looked at his student with compassion and said, "Hasan, keep stirring the halva. When the time comes and you are worthy, you will be both sultan and sovereign. But as you saw, today is not that day." As Salih Usta finished his story, Barış was still stirring his halva.

*"The measure of my merit is to know
that my merit is not enough."*

Saint Augustine

*With the story of the Falcon,
the door opened a little more...*

THE ALBATROSS'S STORY
SUSPICION

"Despair destroys some,
while suspicion destroys everyone."

Benjamin Franklin

Haluk was reviewing the files for the meeting he would attend the next day. This case had turned into a somewhat personal matter since his client was a close friend. He was in an unfamiliar situation, feeling conflicted between his professional attitude and his emotions.

Haluk was not a person who could easily express his emotions. He never cried, even during his days in the orphanage. Almost a quarter-century had passed since then... Now, he was so successful in this life that he started 1-0 behind. Kamuran Bey, a benefactor who stood by him, played a significant role in his achievements. Kamuran provided Haluk with a scholarship, despite not having met him, when he was a young man beginning to embark on a journey because he believed in Haluk's potential. Thanks to Kamuran Bey, Haluk completed high school without worrying about financial problems and graduated from the law faculty with honors.

Haluk felt a sense of peace in having not betrayed the trust placed on him. He never forgot to mention his guardian angel in his prayers. When Haluk started practicing law, he wanted to help financially troubled people for free and eventually actualized this dream. Just as Kamuran Bey had supported him, he never withheld his own support from those in need. But now, for the first time, he took on the case of a close friend. This case was of particular importance to him, and he realized that he was a bit uneasy because of it.

Haluk's friend, Mustafa, worked as a sales manager at a private company. Their paths had crossed during their university years. They shared a house for a while and watched over each other during those challenging years. When they met one day, Mustafa told Haluk that he couldn't stand the injustices he experienced at work anymore and needed his help. Haluk first listened to his friend in order to evaluate the situation. According to Mustafa, the sales director, Burak Bey, was a character who cared about no one but himself. He took on the team's successes as his own while putting the blame for mistakes on someone on the team. As Haluk listened to the stories, he started experiencing a buildup of anger. After all, his intolerance towards injustice was the key reason for choosing his profession. Mustafa, on the other hand, had been fulfilling the tasks given to him meticulously. Moreover, he had prepared a crucial sales proposal for the company during the previous week. However, the sale had not been acknowledged due to errors in the offer, and Mustafa had received a warning based on Burak Bey's report. After arguing with his boss and being subjected to insults, Mustafa decided to take the matter to court. Since the company's human resources department wanted to resolve the issue without going to this measure, Haluk was invited to the office as Mustafa's attorney.

Before speaking with someone from human resources, Haluk met with Burak Bey. Burak turned out to be a very different person than he had imagined. Politely, Burak reminded him that he needed to check his phone during their conversation. Haluk showed understanding. He expected Burak to complain about his client. However, Burak never attempted to do so. Instead, his phone rang persistently several times during their conversation. As far as Haluk could tell, Burak's son had a health problem. When they resumed talking, Burak showed Haluk a report he had compiled on Mustafa's previous work deficiencies. However, the most surprising thing was that these reports had not been shared with upper management before. Haluk, who expected to speak with a monster, was ashamed of his suspicions.

After completing his conversation with Burak, Haluk went to his appointment with Şermin Hanım, the head of human resources. When he entered the room, his eyes were immediately drawn to a bulletin board. On it were photos of sales employees holding their awards. Şermin Hanım explained that the board was prepared to increase the motivation of the staff.

Interestingly, the architect of this system was none other than Burak Bey himself. The fact that Mustafa was not in any of the pictures might have been related to Burak Bey's personal animosity. However, Şermin Hanım quickly disproved this hypothesis, as the voting was done by the employees themselves.

In Haluk's mind, Mustafa and Burak kept transforming into different figures with each passing minute. Still, this could not excuse Burak's offensive behavior. In Haluk's conversation with Şermin Hanım, it was revealed that Burak Bey's son had recently been diagnosed with cancer. The pressure of sales, which was already weighing heavily on Burak Bey, who was usually very polite, had become even more unbearable due to this news.

Haluk found himself in a whirlwind of disarray, with images of Mustafa painted in his mind with brushstrokes, all upside down. In addition to the suspicions Mustafa had created in his head, another party that needed to be blamed was the senior management, who heaped this heavy sales burden on the employees. From the conversation with Şermin Hanım, it was clear that the company's sales expectations had increased due to the effects of the economy. Regardless, treating employees in this manner was inhumane. Unable to contain his anger, Haluk quickly marched to the executive floor. He headed towards the general manager's office. Just as the secretary asked if he had an appointment, the general manager came out of his office. Haluk, with a bold but polite attitude, stated that he wanted to discuss an important issue, and to his surprise, he was met with understanding. Wasn't this man, who resembled an old Istanbul gentleman, actually the one who exploited the employees? Regardless, he had to confront him about this unacceptable behavior. As he entered, trying to control his anger, his eyes caught the nameplate on the president's desk: "Kamuran Atay."

He felt as if boiling water had been poured over him. Because the person he had just angrily restrained himself from lunging at was none other than Kamuran Bey, the angel of goodness...

Haluk realized that he was not alone in crafting a story in his mind, just like Mustafa. In fact, he had also created a scenario of suspicions for himself, just like Mustafa. Real life was filled with various Mustafas, Buraks, Şermins, and Kamurans. What made them heroes or enemies were merely our suspicions, he thought. Mustafa was not only a personality created in Haluk's own world based on his experiences and emotions, but also not the real Mustafa. The more the difference between the two Mustafas, the more disappointment Haluk would feel. He realized that it was necessary to establish relationships with people's realities rather than view others with suspicion and through assumptions, which are not even based on actual facts. We must observe our minds and thoughts with care and clarity.

"Suspicion is slavery."

Things Nobody Can Know - Sinan Canan

When the Albatross completed his story,
the door opened a little wider.

-28-
THE CROW'S STORY
VIGILANCE

"Avoid any environment that does not fill you with truth, do not approach. Empty words are the fire of heedlessness that will burn you. Does regret at the last breath bring any benefit?"

Epictetus

Denise angrily hung up the phone on her friend. Since their school years, she and Melissa had been inseparable. They had argued once over a matter of the heart when they were young, but that was due to their inexperience. Since that day, they had promised each other that no one would come between them. Theirs was such a strong friendship. But this time, Denise was very angry that things had gotten out of hand, and she couldn't accept what Melissa had done. She needed to clear her head urgently. She began to think about what had happened over the past three months...

Everything had started on the day with a car accident, which would be a turning point in her life. Denise was returning to Baltimore from a business trip when she saw a crashed car on the roadside. She had made a habit of choosing the forest road instead of the highway, which was congested during rainfall. Despite the darkness, being familiar with the road had given Denise the courage to speed up a bit. When she quickly pressed on the brakes, the car slid a little due to the rain. Luckily, there was no one coming from behind. She wondered if anyone would pass by at this hour. Then she quickly opened the door and ran towards the crashed car.

The driver was lying motionless in the front. In the back seat, there was a woman and a crying baby in her lap. Denise instinctively took the baby and got out of the car. The woman, whom she later learned was named Lucy, called out to Denise pleadingly: "Please take the baby and get to the hospital urgently. I'm fine, I shouldn't be in this car. Take this as a request from one woman to another... Please don't mention me to anyone. I will take your phone number and call you."

In the shock of the incident and with the instinct to take the baby to a hospital urgently, Denise gave Lucy her phone number and immediately hit the road. The nearest hospital was just north of Baltimore, in the city of Towson. While worrying about the condition of the car driver, whom she had no chance to check on, she saw an ambulance passing by in the opposite direction. It must have been going to Lucy. Denise felt a little relieved, and her only concern now was to get the baby to the hospital on time. The baby was neither crying nor moving. During the drive to the hospital, time passed so slowly and in such a tremendous silence that Denise felt as if she could hear her heart pounding.

Finally, she reached the hospital doors in what felt like the longest journey of her life. She hurriedly handed the baby over to the doctors. She didn't know how much time had passed, and she wasn't aware of how many minutes it took to get there. She was afraid of not being able to give logical answers to the questions asked, but after the first examination, the doctor appeared and gave her the good news. There was nothing to worry about regarding the baby's health. However, the doctor did not hesitate to mention that if she had come later, there could have been permanent damage.

Denise, who had never had children, was experiencing indescribable emotions. At that moment, she noticed the flashing light of her forgotten, silent phone and quickly gathered her strength to answer it. It was Lucy calling, and this woman, whom she had met only two hours ago, was talking to her as if she had known and trusted her for a long time. Lucy told her that the driver was the baby's father and that he had died during the accident. So, there was nothing either woman could do for the father. However, if Denise were to mention that Lucy was in the car during the accident, the consequences would be devastating for a family that had already lost its head.

Denise decided to go along with this solidarity, which seemed like an unwritten rule among women. Lucy couldn't find words to describe the heroism that Denise had shown during the incident. She immediately called a friend who worked at CNN and arranged an interview with Denise. Although Denise was initially hesitant, she eventually gave in to Lucy's insistence.

By then, the baby's mother, Shirley, had arrived at the hospital. After seeing her baby first, she came to meet Denise, who had given her this gift. It was evident from Shirley's demeanor that she was experiencing mixed emotions between the bitterness of losing her husband and the gratitude of seeing her daughter again. The mother hugged Denise, and her tears turned into a downpour of rain. Just then, the journalist that Lucy had mentioned also arrived at the hospital. He didn't miss the opportunity of capturing this striking scene while interviewing Denise.

The next day, Denise appeared in both visual and print media as the leading actor in a heroic story. Melissa was one of the first to congratulate Denise for her actions. Relying on the closeness of their friendship, Melissa mentioned during their conversations that, in fact, any woman could show compassion in such a situation. Denise was bothered by the fact that her close friend did not appreciate her great heroism enough.

Lucy, on the other hand, had been calling Denise regularly since the accident, and they talked at length. She also interpreted Melissa's behavior as jealousy. After all, who was making such sacrifices nowadays? Moreover, Lucy opened new opportunities for Denise to increase her visibility by using her connections. First, she directed a social media influencer to Denise. As a result, Denise quickly increased her social media followers and began receiving offers for television programs due to her newfound fame.

Denise continued to regularly communicate by phone with Lucy, whom she had never met face-to-face since the accident and generally sought advice from her. From her clothes and accessories to her hair color and handbag style, Denise now acted under Lucy's guidance. This change was not well-received by Melissa at all. Jealousy had turned these old friends into strangers. Worse still, Melissa wasn't the only one reacting negatively to Denise's transformation. Their mutual friends were also unhappy with the change. The helpful and humble woman they once knew was no longer present.

The new Denise began her day by checking her follower count on social media. She calculated the number of followers and likes, and on days when her expectations were not met, she experienced fits of rage. On the other hand, to further increase her fame, she considered the TV show offers made to her with Lucy's help and thought she could make good money from this. She found the first offer insufficient. Later, she agreed to a show after negotiations but caused great trouble for the producers. A program was planned within a script framework featuring the baby and its mother, Shirley, who had earned her this fame. Shirley was delighted with the idea of doing a program together with Denise, whom she saw as a hero for her family. However, she found a completely different Denise. This new Denise couldn't even bear the baby's crying, which she had brought to the hospital with a mother's compassion. Her rude behavior towards Shirley greatly upset the mother. As a result, the program lacked sincerity.

Denise had made it a habit to tell Lucy about similar daily events under the title of daily complaints, and fall into a slumber of heedlessness by listening to the lullaby Lucy sang for her ego. Within a few weeks, Lucy's TV show was canceled first. The rapidly spreading "problematic" reputation in the market had put a barrier in front of any other program offers. Denise had quit her routine jobs to make money, trusting in her story and Lucy, and had gone into debt to create her new image. Now, as the news about her in the press decreased, her fame began to fade, and this was reflected in her social media. Thus, under the shadow of the darkness that had settled upon her life, she found her solution in seeking Melissa. But the things Melissa said to turn her back into the Denise she knew had long gone in one ear and out the other, and eventually, Melissa had to say she would not deal with this new Denise.

Although Denise was very angry during her conversation with Melissa, when she calmed down a bit, she realized that this anger was actually towards herself, not Melissa. When she analyzed the past three months with a cool head, she realized that since meeting Lucy, the only thing that had grown in her life was her ego. It was as if a court had been set up inside her, and she was on trial. The people she had hurt appeared before her one by one... The only testimony she could give was about how regretful she was. However, she had an instigator, and she had to call and immediately cut ties with her...

Without wasting time, she grabbed her phone, but received a message that the number she was calling was not in use. In the meantime, she noticed that she had placed Lucy at the top of her quick dial. Maybe she had canceled her phone or changed her number. They had mutual acquaintances anyway. She called the CNN reporter whom Lucy had contacted on the day of the accident. The reporter said he didn't have a friend named Lucy. He explained that he came to the hospital to visit a friend that day, and their encounter was purely coincidental.

She couldn't comprehend this... In shock, this time she called the social media influencer who was famous and had helped Lucy. She explained that she had seen her on the news and was very impressed, so she contacted her. "I don't know the person named Lucy you mentioned," she finished.

Denise held her head with both hands and struggled with the pain that pierced her head as she tried to digest her experiences. At that moment, the doorbell rang. A private messenger brought Denise a letter. Our hero tore open the envelope and began reading the letter addressed to her.

"Dear Denise,

First of all, thank you for inviting me into your life. In return for this invitation, I have only fulfilled your wishes. Since the day I met you, I have introduced you to people who added fame to your fame, made you money, and saved you from people who were unworthy of you. However, I see that you are not very satisfied with your life. Know that I have never said anything other than what you wanted to hear. I can only whisper into the ears of those who want to listen. We call this heedlessness, dear sister... Where I come from, there is always fire but no wood. Everyone collects their own wood during the time of heedlessness and brings it along. I hope to see you again soon. Lucy..."

"What one does to oneself, one finds and suffers;
remember that. Gaining takes a whole lifetime, while
losing takes just a moment of heedlessness."

Mevlana Jalaluddin Rumi

When the Crow finished the story,
the door opened a little wider.

29

THE NIGHTINGALE'S STORY
FORGIVENESS

"Forgiveness is the attribute of the strong."

Mahatma Gandhi

Since last night, the inhabitants of the house had been trying to put the upside-down house back in order. But what was turned upside down was not just the items in the house... Although the father of the house, Metin Bey, had maintained his composure despite everything, his elder son Kerem could not accept his father's attitude towards the events and had left the house by slamming the door. The youngest of the house, Sinan, didn't think what his brother did was right, but he also couldn't digest his father's indifference.

If we go back to last night, Metin Bey's house had been targeted by two thieves. The fact that no one, except the house steward Kâmil Bey, knew the family would be attending a long-planned dinner, had cast suspicion on the steward. The thieves had effortlessly entered the house and spent their time recklessly gathering almost all the valuable items as if they had placed them there themselves. According to the police report, the thieves had immediately neutralized the steward upon entering the house and had tied his hands and feet.

The unexpected illness of the mother of the house had caused the family dinner to be very short and the family members to return home earlier than expected. Thus, the two young men in their mid-20s had been caught red-handed without a chance to escape. This was an easy scenario to solve for both the police and the homeowners, and the main suspect was the house steward. When Kerem overcame the shock of the incident, he immediately confronted the steward. His father stopped him and told him to control his anger. He then sent him to the back room with his brother Sinan while he himself dealt with the police officers.

When the police commissioner mentioned that he also suspected the steward and that they could easily get the thieves to confess through interrogation, Metin Bey said he would not accuse his 40-year employee. He also stated that he forgave the thieves and, while knowing it would be a public case, he would not file a complaint. After the police left the house, Kerem also left the house, thinking that what his father had done was wrong. Sinan was still trying to digest the events. As he wondered how he could live under the same roof with Kâmil now, Metin Bey invited Sinan to a private conversation and told him the following story:

"During the Prophet Moses' journey to the Canaan lands, he faced a prolonged drought in one region. He went to pray for rain with those nearby, asking for God's help. However, instead of rain, an even hotter air descended from the darkened sky. It was revealed to the bewildered Moses that there was a sinner among the Jews. This person had been defying God for 40 years, and God would not bestow His mercy until this person left the crowd. Moses called out to the people, asking the sinner to come forward. But no one spoke up... At that moment, the sinful person was gripped with immense fear. If he didn't come forward, the people would perish from thirst; if he did, he would be cursed by the people for the rest of his life. In this remorse, he begged for forgiveness from God with such a heartfelt plea that the sound of the lightning in his heart drowned out the voices in the sky. Then a torrential rain began. While the Jewish people were overjoyed, Moses was puzzled by the situation. He appealed to God, asking who the sinful person was. God said that this servant had been gossiping about Him for 40 years and was, therefore, in sin, but He had accepted the heartfelt forgiveness he had asked for. Nevertheless, the final message to Moses in this story was, 'Should I gossip about him by revealing his name to you, O Prophet?'

Sinan understood that his father had forgiven his 40-year-old loyal servant, sins and all, and had covered his sin. However, he could not forgive the crime committed by someone who had been eating their bread for so long. Metin Bey empathized with his son's feelings while also wanting to explain to him that anyone could fall into such a situation. He continued the conversation with another story:

"During the time of the Prophet Jesus, a woman was caught committing adultery and was awaiting the punishment to be handed down. According to Jewish laws, the punishment for this crime was death by stoning. They consulted Jesus' opinion to test whether he would adhere to the ancient laws, as he had always emphasized forgiveness in his sermons. The Prophet Jesus requested that they move to a larger area for the execution of the woman's punishment. The crowd gathered, each person picking up one or two stones.

However, Jesus said something the people did not expect: 'Let the one who is without sin cast the first stone!' Starting with the elders, the group that had assembled for the execution began to drop their stones and leave the area. When no one was left, Jesus asked the woman, 'Has no one condemned you?' The woman replied, 'No one, my Lord...' The final words of the Prophet Jesus were, 'Then neither do I condemn you; I forgive you. Go and sin no more.'"

After hearing the story, Sinan slumped in his seat. All the injustices he had done to others flashed before his eyes one by one. As if dropping an imaginary stone from his hand, he clung to his father's hands and asked for his own forgiveness. His anger had given way to compassion. Because he had forgiven, this time he had truly forgiven...

His father looked at him with a smile and ended the conversation with the famous words of Nelson Mandela, the renowned statesman who had become a symbol of Africa, on the day he was released from prison after 27 years:

"As I walked out the door toward my freedom,
I knew that if I did not leave my bitterness and
hatred behind, I would still be in prison."

As the Nightingale finished its story,
the door opened a little wider.

30

THE PARROT TUTI'S STORY
SINCERITY

E ren was just about to turn three years old when Cengo pawed his way through the door. Cengiz and Gonca had thought long and hard about the pros and cons of bringing a dog into their home for Eren. But the story Gonca's father told them made their decision much easier.

The great Sufi mystic Muhyiddin Ibn Arabi had spent most of his life as a wanderer. On one of his journeys, he found himself in a wooded area. As he searched for a place to rest, he noticed frightened animals fleeing away from him, startled by the sound of crushed branches beneath his feet. Ibn Arabi convinced himself that it was only natural for these wild animals to react in such a manner. Then, while he was reading, his eyes caught sight of the sandals on his feet. He wondered how much this piece of leather separated him from the earth, the origin of everything. He thought about how the animals he had just labeled as wild never severed their connection with the earth. Indeed, it was not the animals but humans who were truly wild, he thought to himself. The more the connection with nature was broken, the less humanity remained...

After listening to this story, the young parents took a syllable from each of their names and named their baby Golden, Cengo. Cengo, one of the best breeds for getting along with children, quickly became Eren's most loyal friend over the years. The two grew up together, never hesitating to show their love for one another.

On Eren's first day of school, his friendliness toward his classmates made Cengiz very happy. Another unique trait of Eren was his ability to create paintings with skill beyond his age. Gonca soon noticed her son's extraordinary talent and encouraged him. That year, for Mother's Day, Eren painted a picture of his mother as the best gift he could give her. His tiny heart must have been pounding like Leonardo da Vinci's when he put the final brushstroke on the Mona Lisa. Just then, Cengo, perhaps out of animal instinct or jealousy - of the love between mother and son, sank his teeth into the freshly painted picture. Before Gonca could comprehend what had happened, both the painting and Eren's tiny heart were shattered. For the next two days, Eren did not allow the Golden, who was accustomed to sleeping at the foot of his bed, into his room. However, on the third day, the little boy succumbed to his old friend's charm. Cengo's embarrassment was evident as he looked up from beneath Eren's arm, capturing his friend's gaze. When he made Eren laugh, it was as if he had conquered the world...

A few months later, Cengo suddenly fell ill with an unexpected disease. The veterinarian said it was a genetic kidney disorder. For the first time in his short life, Eren experienced the pain of saying goodbye to a loved one. Overwhelmed with grief, the child locked himself in his room. Both Cengiz and Gonca prayed for their son's justifiable and silent outcry to end.

At the end of an emotionally turbulent week, Eren came to his mother with a piece of paper in his hand. From the outside, it seemed to be a letter. As his mother couldn't hide her surprise, an even stranger request came from the little boy. Eren asked his mother for God's address to complete his letter. Gonca, perhaps in an effort to control the impact of this potentially pivotal moment in her son's life, convinced herself that it was right to participate in his imaginative game. She took the letter, saying she would deliver it to its owner, and read it through tears:

"Dear God. I am Eren. Cengo is my dog. My mother told me he went to be with you. You are very good, but you have a lot of work. Can he sleep in your room in the evenings? He won't make any noise, don't worry. I will pray to you every evening if you take care of him until I arrive. Please write to me. Eren."

Gonca put the letter in an envelope in front of Eren's eyes. She would continue this game. She immediately jumped into her car and headed for the post office, or at least that's what Eren would think. As she circled around the house, her thoughts circled around her mind. If a dictionary were to provide a definition of love, they could put this little child's letter as an example, she thought with a strange sense of peace. When she returned home, she answered Eren's excited gaze with the demeanor of a dutiful official who had done her job without a flaw, nodding her head up and down. After all, school would end in a week, and the summer vacation would begin. She would find a way to handle the rest if she could keep Eren occupied until then. The next day, as the family was about to sit down for dinner, the doorbell rang. An unusual postman arrived at an unexpected time, holding a letter in his hand. "For Mr. Eren..." he said as he handed over the entrusted letter. The evening darkness was about to descend, but the postman's face seemed to light up the entire room. Eren could only make out the large letter "C" on the cap of the person handing him the letter. He began to read the lines...

"Dear Eren. I received your letter. Let me share a secret with you. I was Cengo's owner before you. You took great care of him; thank you. He has now returned home and is sleeping in his room. Don't worry at all. He asked me to send you a gift. You painted a picture for your mother. He accidentally tore it. We are sending it back to you. I will listen to your prayers every evening."

When Eren unfolded the attached and folded paper, he saw the picture he had made for his mother. However, there was a Cengo that was not in the original picture but was still drawn by his own hand at his mother's feet. He was smiling and very happy...

*"A wise person understands that sincerity
is the most powerful force in the world
and becomes its ally."*

Frank Crane

*When Tuti's story ended, the door moved
one last time and opened completely...*

FINAL CURTAIN

The door of Qaf was fully open now. The birds were motionless and no longer had the strength to move. As they remembered the friends they had lost along the way, they tried to muster the energy to flap their wings a few more times. Their bodies were exhausted. Hoopoe was aware that he had reached the final stage of his unwavering guidance. With a final effort, he entered, and the others followed their guide as they had done from the beginning.

The birds found themselves in a new, colorless, and odorless valley. A horizon appeared before them where the concrete flowed towards the abstract and vanished from sight. Right on the horizon, they saw a curtain that seemed to embrace the sky as if it stretched to infinity. The birds were now aware that this was the final curtain between them and the Simurgh. When they felt to their very core that life was no different from a theater, they understood that they needed to play the final curtain in the best way possible. The only key to this was for each bird to play its role according to the name it was created for.

The birds flapped their wings until they reached the enormous, glistening curtain. At this point, all of them would display their skills in such a way that the 30 birds together would accomplish what a single skill could not. As the Dove put it, one last service was needed. First, the Hawk faced the door of Qaf and closed it with all its might, never to open it again. The birds no longer had ties to the world. As the Stork put it, they had left the transience of the fleeting world behind. Thanks to the Nightingale, the birds forgave all the siblings who had abandoned them on the journey they had started together. The Parakeet had brought together these remaining 30 birds in Friendship, conveying the sincerity and compassion they felt for each other, which the little Finch also emphasized. This made them, in the words of the Robin, the most blessed community in the universe.

Then the Raven made a move to form a circle around their guide, the Hoopoe. Reality had to be a system with Goodness at its core. At that moment, the Rookie extended its wing to the Raven to connect to the system with harmony; for this to work, the birds had to surrender to their central guide without any doubt in their hearts. All the birds had already passed the loyalty test under the leadership of the Turtle Dove. The Falcon testified that each bird deserved a place in this circle. Now each of them, like the Crow, had completely awoken from his or her heedlessness and individuated selves.

The Seagull soared and showed all the birds their proper places from her bird's-eye view. The Eagle ensured that each bird was positioned at an equal distance from the central guide. Even though their characteristics were different, Justice required every bird to remain at an equal distance from each other. However, the Peacock did not observe this equality in the distances between the birds themselves, placing them at different distances from each other. Each bird's characteristics were relative to the others.

The Owl suggested all the Birds turn their faces towards their Guide, the Hoopoe. It knew that true Wisdom came from the Guide. The Pelican asked that all the birds lower and bow their heads until they completely overcame the last hint of their pride. Its sibling, the Swallow, also assisted with its quality of spiritual determination. At last, all the birds bowed humbly before their guide as the Canary, and the Hawk announced the news that they had all regained their True Freedom.

When the Flamingo joined the ceremony, the Hoopoe began to whirl in the center, with all the birds spinning, like constellations, harmoniously around him. As the Robin described, this Unity was so perfect that it seemed as if all the birds were connected by invisible threads. Under the leadership of the Swan, the birds entered the Flow, and individual movements began to disappear. As the Pheasant pointed out, the only thing noticeable from the outside was the presence and order of Unity. All the birds realized, with the help of the Eagle Owl, that they had become One Being.

The spinning speed was increasing steadily. The Partridge sensed that an end was near and was aware that a Sacrifice was still necessary. It was time for all the birds to *die*. The mass that had become one body burst into flames. The fire suddenly leapt onto the curtain, and the curtain began to burn along with the birds. Before dying, the birds would be able to see the Simurgh behind the curtain as it burned. At that moment, the Albatross heard the voice of the Simurgh. *"My birds! If you try to see Me before you die, I will only be what you think I am. But if you die in yourselves and come to life in Me, then you can see the Real Me."*

When the curtain had burned completely, they saw that behind it was only a mirror, and there was nothing on it but their reflections. The Crane shouted "Unity!" and all the birds surrendered their souls. Now, neither the Hoopoe nor any other bird's body remained. Only their ashes, indistinguishable from one another, floated in the air. Then the ashes slowly merged.

At last, the Simurgh appeared, with wings so vast that they nearly shadowed the sun. Behind the burnt curtain, in the mirror, the Simurgh gazed at its own Beauty; in our language, "Si" means "thirty" and "Murg" means "bird." Thirty birds passed away and were reborn in the Simurgh. God is a Treasure who loves to be *known*.

"The mind that rules alone is a limiting power; passion left unbridled is a flame that burns until it destroys itself. Therefore, let your soul elevate your mind to the peaks of passion to sing. Let your soul guide your passion with reason, so that your passion may be reborn daily like the phoenix from its ashes. You must dwell in reason and move with passion."

The Prophet – Khalil Gibran

AFTERWORD:
THE STORY OF HOW THESE STORIES CAME TO BE PUBLISHED IN KENTUCKY!

Yes, behind all stories are many other stories.

How did I meet Kerim Guc? In 2011, Fons Vitae had just published Listen: Commentary on the Spiritual Couplets of Mevlana Rumi , working long distance with our Kenan Rifai friends, never imagining we would ever meet our invisible colleagues in person. Several years later, we were traveling with Kentucky friends visiting Greece and Turkey. Before leaving America, we let our Listen family know of our coming and a dinner was arranged for our last evening in Istanbul. When we entered the restaurant, I was surprised to see a large group of young people seated around a long table – having previously imagined our associates were more our age – or older. During the course of dinner, I complained to the group about the way the local tour guides presented the sites to our group. I had so looked forward to sharing – with my many dear friends on this trip – the spiritual dimension of Turkey, its art, architecture, places like Mary's house in Ephesus, Turkey's sacred history and culture. But the guides ruined it, seemingly having had a secular upbringing or education. I expressed how sad I was that this spiritual dimension seemed less evident, for the most part, in the country today. Instantly, someone exclaimed, pointing to Kerim, who was 39 years old at the time, "But the mother of Kerim Guc, here, is a living saint in Istanbul – even speaking often on TV!" I asked him if there were a way Fons

Vitae could publish something she wrote, translated into English, always delighted to have more titles on women's spirituality, of which there are too few.

With the help of many fine editors, a translation of Beauty and Light: Mystical Discourses by a Contemporary Female Sufi Master, came out in 2018. I had the privilege of meeting Cemalnur Sargut when she addressed students in Chapel Hill at the University of North Carolina, arranged by Professor Omid Safi, a member of Fons Vitae's Scholarly Board. As she spoke, she radiated and literally embodied pure Joy and Love. I fell in love with her luminous Happiness.

Later, I visited Cemalnur in Istanbul. As she prepared breakfast (she is an extraordinary cook), she told me the following story , which I never forgot. When her father had once been imprisoned, she rushed to her mother's side in tears. "Alhamdulillah," her mother counseled, "your father has been given the blessing of sharing in the same trial as our Prophet Joseph." When I heard this, my perspective on scripture and sacred stories was transformed. When we hear what trials have been endured by prophets such as Jonah, Jesus, Buddha, Muhammed, and in the endless lives of saints, we are being given archetypes. When a trial takes over any one of our lives, we have role models to follow, which demonstrate how these exemplary beings handled what they had to confront. If enormous patience is required, we need only recall the example of Job for both perspective and guidance. It has been said that when a trial occurs, we need to say "Praise the Lord, it could have been worse. Praise the Lord, this happened to my body and not my soul, and Al-hamdullilah, it happened in this world and not the Next."

In time, Fons Vitae also had the honor of co-publishing the extraordinary work, O Humankind: Surah Ya Sin , which arose from Cemalnur Sargut and her colleagues spending 5 years discussing a wealth of profound commentaries on this surah, by some of the greatest spiritual authorities.

Over time, when I visited Istanbul, Kerim generously accompanied me on visits to such precious long-time friends as Mahmud Erol Kilic and Shems Friedlander, may he rest in peace. Recently, Kerim introduced me to fellow lovers of Ghazali, Ercument and Ikbal Tokat, who have kindly made this present volume possible, and with whom I share so much. This includes our common concern for the education of the children in the Syrian refugee camps – where the Tokat family have already done more good than is imaginable.

Kentucky has also been honored to receive both Kerim and his mother as participants and speakers in our annual Festival of Faiths (2018), put on by the Center for Interfaith Relations. To think that they too have visited my home territory! (See footage of precious Cemalnur speaking: https://www. centerforinterfaithrelations.org/past-festivals/2018-festival-of-faiths/)

So, look at how the Divine Plan brought a group of us together, as a "Team." Imagine that Fons Vitae, which traditionally only publishes translations of classical manuscripts from the world's spiritual heritage, has now begun to welcome offerings from a new and younger generation of scholars and seekers, making their way from "I" to "Him."

We are delighted for our small part in helping to share the stories which have meant so much to the son of Cemalnur Sargut. We all know what an influence parents are on their children.

Gray Henry
Director of Fons Vitae